The Horrors of Salem's
WITCH DUNGEON

*This book is dedicated to Robert Curran, James Marks, and James Hurrell, of Salem, Marblehead, and North Andover, Massachusetts, three men from **witch country**, who had faith enough to believe that a Salem Witch could really fly.*

Condemned witches leave Salem's Witch Dungeon for Gallows Hill.
Sketch by Trish Cahill.

Cover Photos: ISBN 0-916787-08-7

Puritans in pillory and stocks at Salem's Pioneer Village, photo courtesy Henry Theriault, Sea-Witch, Salem, MA; Display of life-size clay figures in stocks and behind bars, courtesy Witch Dungeon Museum, Salem, MA; Accused witches in cart, and drummers with teamsters at the hanging tree, from the television mini-series, *"Three Sovereigns For Sarah,"* courtesy Nightowl Productions, Nahant, MA; Howard Street Burial Ground behind the Salem Jail, and two witches hanging at Gallows Hill, photos by the author; Hanging of Sarah Good, on ladder with hangman, from *"Three Sovereigns For Sarah,"* photo by Mikki Ansin, Cambridge, MA.

INTRODUCTION

In 1973, I was elected High Sheriff of Essex County, Massachusetts, with added duties as Master and Keeper of the Salem Jail & House of Correction. This decrepid bastile that houses over 200 inmates, or *"residents"* as they are called today, was built in 1813. Referred to then as the *"new stone goal"*, it was constructed to replace the former wooden structure, known as *the "Witch Jail"*. The dimensions of the Witch Jail, old records reveal, was *"thirteen feet stud and twenty feet square; "* not much room to house the 150-plus victims of the notorious witch hysteria of 1692. There was, however, a stone dungeon located in the cellar of the Witch Jail, which was rediscovered in 1957 when the land there was excavated to build a New England Telephone Company office building. Retrieved from the remains of the old Witch-Dungeon were a few oak beams. Two of these rare artifacts are displayed at Salem's Essex Institute and at the recreated Witch Dungeon Museum in Salem.

Prior to the building of the Essex County Witch Jail & Dungeon in 1684, Salem had an even smaller jail built in 1636, but as the records reveal, *"it was a mere dwelling near the North River."* The Courthouse, where most of the accused witches were tried, was torn down long ago. It stood near the Witch Jail in the middle of town, at the corner of what is now Washington and Lynde Streets. By coincidence, the recently built Salem District Court stands but a few feet from this original court, and less than 100 yards from the Witch Dungeon Museum. The Witch House, where Jonathan Corwin, one of the witch-hanging judges lived, and Salem's Witch Museum, are only a few blocks away from this once active site of torment and treachery.

My position as Master & Keeper of the Salem Jail, prompted me to dig into the records of my predecessors, where I discovered many brutal, often bizarre, and sometimes humorous incidents concerning the crimes and punishments of our New England ancestors. Their religious prejudices, restrictive laws and ancient superstitions, produced decades of torture and terror that culminated at Salem. When this period was over, there came seventy-seven years of humility and penance: The Essex Gazette of November 12, 1771 reports that, *"Today Bryan Sheehan is convicted of rape. He is the first person convicted of Felony in this large County, since the memorable year 1692, commonly called the Witch Time."* Thus, it was this climax of cruelty by our Puritan forefathers at Salem, that *"turned the world upside down,"* but fortunately seemed to put America back on the right footing.

Bob Cahill

I
PUNISHING PILGRIMS AND PURITANS

In Merry Old England during the late sixteenth and early seventeenth centuries, Pilgrims and Puritans were considered *"dissidents"*. They were often exiled, thrown in jail, harrassed, tortured, and in 1575, the Archbishop of Canterbury had two of them burned alive at the stake. These two groups of dissidents, although not overly fond of each other, and opposed to all other forms of religion, were especially critical of the Church of England, which was the root from which their seperatist beliefs stemmed. Although neither Pilgrim nor Puritan ministers were allowed to preach in England, a Church of England minister, Dr. Laurence Chaderton, who had converted to Puritanism in 1578, gave a sermon at Cambridge which adequately summerized the feelings of the dissidents towards the controlling Church of England: *"The church is a huge mass of old and stinking works,"* Chaderton preached, *"of conjuring, witchcraft, sorcery, blaspheming, swearing and foreswearing, profaning of the Lord's Sabboths, disobediance to superiors, contempt of inferiors, manslaughterers, murderers, robberies, adultery, fornication, false-witness-bearing and lying . . .".* This is the basic feeling of the Pilgrims when they came to settle at Plymouth in 1620, and of the Puritans, when they settled at Salem, Charlestown and Boston in 1630. Dr. Laurence Chaderton, by the way, went on to write the King James version of the Bible.

Of the so-called Pilgrims that came ashore at Plymouth from the Mayflower in December, 1620, only 41 of the 98 were Pilgrims, or *"Saints"* as they called themselves. The others were either servants or Anglicans — Church of England settlers. The Pilgrims were more tolerant of Anglicans than the Puritans were, but whenever there was trouble at Plymouth, an Anglican was usually blamed. *"There are thieves among us,"* Plymouth's Governor Bradford wrote to friends in England, *"but if England had been free from that crime, then we should not have been troubled with these here."* One Anglican-Pilgrim named John Oldham was so outspoken against the *"Saints"* and their strict ways, that, after a brutal beating *"with birch branches and musket butts,"* he was forced to shove off from shore in a little boat, banned from Plymouth, with no other settlement to go to — he drifted to Nantasket and founded what is now Hull, Massachusetts. Following him soon after in exile from Plymouth, was the Pilgrim minister, John Lyford, who was a converted Episcopalian. He was tried at Plymouth for *"disturbing the peace"* and for writing some twenty letters back to England, *"full of slander and false accusations,"* wrote Governor

Bradford. In one of them, he called Miles Standish, military leader of Plymouth, *"a silly boy"*. It was Standish who confiscated the letters by sailing out in his sloop to overtake the ship that was delivering them to England. Also, Lyford's wife told Bradford that he had *"wronged her before marriage"* and that after marriage, her husband had been *"meddling with maids,"* so Lyford was sent off to fish with Oldham at Nantasket.

There was a firebug in Plymouth in 1621, and many of the newly built homes and stables were burnt to the ground by this mysterious person. It was thought to be a servant girl, or possibly John Billington, an Anglican-Pilgrim, who earlier helped start a mutiny aboard the Mayflower. Although the firebug was never caught, he or she succeeded in burning down almost half the dwelling houses within a two year period. Bradford never accused Billington, but did mention in his Journal that Billington and his wife were, *"one of ye profanest families"* in the new settlement. In 1622, for cursing Miles Standish, John Billington was *"tied up by neck and heels"* for almost a full day, until the blood dripped from his nose and eyes. John Billington continued in his belligerent ways for eight more years, until he was hanged for murder at Plymouth on September 30, 1630, the very day that Governor John Winthrop and his Puritans moved in to settle Boston. Reverend Reyner, pastor of the Pilgrim church at Plymouth, resigned his post a few years later and went to Dover, New Hampshire to live, stating his reason that the Pilgrim Fathers *"are too strict in their laws and punishments,"* but if Reyner found the Pilgrims too strict, he would have found the Puritans intolerable.

Only two months after the Puritans arrived in Boston, a man was tied to the whipping-cart and given twenty stripes, for stealing a piece of bread, and another was *"whipt for shooting birds"*. That same day, November 30, 1630, a new Bostonian, *"John Pease, is whipt for striking his mother."* A whipping-cart was found in every village and town in New England in the early 1600s. In the larger towns, it was soon replaced by the whipping-post, usually located in the marketplace near the meetinghouse or jail. Next to the whipping cart or post, were stocks and pillories, slabs of thick wood with half circles cut into them, that, when locked together, made holes for hands, feet, and sometimes head, where a victim would have to stand or sit immobile for hours, occassionally with his or her ears pinned to the wood. Nathaniel Hawthorne, Salem's famous novelist, describes the pillory in "The Scarlet Letter", as *"a penal machine, which was held in the old time to be as effectual in the promotion of good citizenship as ever was the guillotine among the terrorists of France. It was, in short, the platform of the pillory; and above it rose the framework of that instrument of discipline, so fashioned as to confine the human head in its tight grasp, and thus hold it up to the public gaze."*

In Boston, the first person to sit in the stocks as a punishment, was the carpenter who built them. When the magistrates saw Edward Palmer's bill for material and labor of one pound 13 shillings, they fined him five pounds *"and censured him to be set an hour in the stocks."* Next in the Boston stocks was James Luxford, *"to set for two hours for having two wives, and is fined 100 pounds".* The third victim in the stocks was the night watchman — our earliest version of the policeman — *"for being drunk while on duty".*

Diarist Samuel Breck left a brief description of one of Boston's first pillories which was located on King Street: *"There were three or four fellows fastened by the head and hands,"* he writes, *"and standing for an hour in that helpless posture, exposed to gross and cruel jeers from the multitude, who pelted them constantly with rotten eggs and every repulsive kind of garbage that could be collected".* Thomas Scott was placed in the pillory for falsely accusing someone else of a theft. Journalist Henry Brooks tells us that Scott *"was greeted on his appearance by a large mob with a discharge of small shot, such as rotten eggs, filth, and dirt from the streets, which was followed up by dead cats and rats".*

The first to stand in the newly built pillory at Hartford, Connecticut was Nicholas Olmstead, his crime not recorded, yet he was forced *"on next Thursday, to be sent on a little before the beginning of the lecture, and to stay thereon a little after the end."* The Boston magistrates warned the towns of Dedham, Watertown, Concord and Newbury in 1638, to contruct stocks, or pay a fine. They all quickly complied, and less than an hour after the stocks were constructed at Newbury, John Perry was sitting in them, *"for abusing his wife and child."* Four years later, Rehoboth, Massachusetts complied with the law to construct stocks for the unruly, and its first guest was a man the Town Fathers had captured, who was accused of kidnapping an Indian boy. Plymouth, of course, was the first to construct stocks in New England, and the first two victims were women: *"Jane Boulton to sit in the stocks for reviling the magistrates,"* and *"Ann Savory, placed in the stocks for having an unsavory memory."*

The pillory, whipping-post and stocks were used to varying degrees for all sorts of offences: lying, forging, card playing, slander, selling rotten food, overpricing, purse-snatching, drunkeness, unruliness, fighting and brawling, husbands for beating wives, wives for scolding their husbands, swearing and cursing, blasphemy, disobeying Sabbath laws and fortune telling. Often innocent people were *"knocked from pillory to post,"* just because someone thought they might be guilty. At Boston in 1679, eighty waterfront warehouses went up in flames. A local merchant accused a visiting Frenchman of starting the blaze, but there was no proof. In those days, however, all Frenchmen in New England were under suspicion. Without trial, the Frenchman was forced to stand in the pillory, had both his ears cut off, paid a 500 pound fine, and was sent to jail, yet he was never found guilty of starting the fires.

Whipping or *"scourging"* as they sometimes called it, was one of the most common punishments in New England, especially for vagrants, slanderous women and thieves. The long horse-hide whip, usually knotted with three cords at the end to break the victim's skin on impact, was kept at the ready by the County Sheriff or the Town Constable. Their orders from the magistrates were plain enough: *"Vagrants shall be carried to market areas, and there, tied to the end of a cart naked, and beaten with the whip throughout such market town, or other place, till the body shall be bloody by reason of such whipping"*. At Plymouth in 1636, John Billington's wife Helen was *"whipt for slander"*.

Puritan Salem, 1637 — *"Dorothy Talby, for beating her husband, to be bound and chained to a post and be whipped"*. Salem, January, 1642: *"Mary Oliver presented to the magistrates for neglect of public worship"*. Two years later, February, 1644, *"Mary Oliver, publicly whipped for reproaching the magistrates"*. On August 12, 1646, *"Mary Oliver to have a cleft stick put on her tongue for half an hour for slander"*. The last mention of Mary in the Essex County court records, is March, 1647: *"Mary Oliver, to be whipt and banished from Salem Towne"*. One wonders, what ever happened to dear old Mary Oliver.

Peddlers wandering from one New England village to another in the late 1600s, selling their wares, became an economic threat to local shopkeepers. They were often arrested by Constables, stripped naked, flogged through the village streets and ordered never to return, or they would face worse punishment. Even in the most liberal communities, such as Westerly, Rhode Island, where outcasts from Puritan and Pilgrim societies had settled, strict laws against Vagrants and peddlers were passed by the Town Fathers — *"that the officer shall take the said transient forthwith to some publick place in this Towne and strip him from the waist upward, and whip him twenty stripes, well layed on his naked back, and then be by said officer, transported out of this Town"*. The whipping-post at Westerly was an old tree located just outside the door of Gavitt Tavern. At Providence, Rhode Island at the turn of the century, a Mr. Channing informs us that vagabond-peddlers not only suffered the whip, but often the added harrassment from onlookers: *"The neck of the culprit was bent to a most uncomfortable curve,"* writes Channing, *"presenting a facial mark for those salutations of stale eggs which seemed to have been preserved for the occasion. The place selected for the infliction of this punishment was in front of the State House"*.

At neighboring Connecticut, the whip was also the favorite tool of discipline. The first settlers at New Haven explained in writing that *"stripes and whippings is a creation fit and proper in some cases where offense is accompanied with childish or brutal folly, or rudeness, or with stubborn insolency or beastly cruelty, or with idle vagrancy, or for faults to like nature"*. At Hartford, Connecticut, on May 12, 1668, Mary Wilton was stripped naked before a mob of hecklers and strapped to the whipping-post. The court record reads: *"Nicholas Wilton, for wounding the wife of John Brooks, and Mary Wilton the wife of Nicholas, for contemptious and reproachful terms by her on one of the assistants, are adjudged she be whipt six stripes upon her naked body next training day at Windsor, and the said Nicholas is hereby disfranchised of his freedom in this Corporation, and to pay for the Horse and Man that came with him to the Court, and for what damage he has done to the said Brooks, his wife, and sit in the stocks the same day his wife is to receive her punishment"*. Nowhere in the court record does it explain what Nicholas and Mary Wilton did to John Brooks and his wife, but usually when sins or crimes go unexplained in old town records, one can guess the manner of the crime.

Whipping as a punishment to seamen, sometimes for minor infractions aboard ship, was second only to drowning as a constant fear. One lash from a *"cat-o-nine tails"* would severely bruise and often break the skin. The regulation twelve lashes from the long whip with nine pieces of line spliced into it and Turk's-Head knots on the ends, would make the victim's back look like roasted meat. Three dozen lashes would often kill the victim. Yet, some New England seamen have been known to withstand 100 or more lashes from the *cat-o-nine tails*. Often it was the strength and dexterity of the man wielding the whip that saved or killed an unfortunate seaman. One Boston merchant-marine who experienced a flogging aboard a British ship, wrote in his diary that, *"after two or three strokes the pain in my lungs was more severe, I thought, than on my* back. I felt as if I would burst in the internal parts of my body... I put my tongue between my teeth, held it there, and bit it in almost two pieces... I was almost choked with blood and became black in the face...". Floggings aboard vessels remained routine procedure well into the nineteenth century.

Our forefathers as children in Puritanical New England, were also in constant fear of the whip. Not only schoolmasters, but strict parents, and even local ministers, were constantly ready with the whip or rod, *as not to spoil the child.* One of the Pilgrim's first ministers at Plymouth, Jonathan Edwards, was notorious for his heavy, whipwielding hand, especially to disruptive little boys. He once preached to the Pilgrims that, *"boys are infinitely more hateful to God than vipers".* Henry Brooks of Boston writes that, *"the beating of scholars is a practice very common in schools here, for such offenses as whispering and looking off the book. I know a master whose delight, apparently, was pounding and beating little boys. He did not touch the large ones, and yet, he was considered a first rate teacher".* A Colonial law in Boston read: *"All idle persons and boys who throw snowballs shall be whipped".* Also in Boston, in 1725, a 16 year old boy, *"for abusing smaller children, is sentenced 39 stripes at the cart tail, 12 at the gallows, 13 at the head of Summer Street, 13 below the town-houses, and be committed to Bridewell for six months".*

At that same time, Sarah Emery of Newbury, Massachusetts, writes that, *"my cousin Moses Smith, a poor little puny boy of five, but of delicate and amiable disposition, had a wholesome dread of School Master Joseph Adams. When school was dismissed, the little boy was retained... and after a while I espied Moses creeping up the lane... I ran to him, and with a piteous moan he sank fainting into my arms. My cries aroused the family. The child was taken to the house, and the physician summoned. Consciousness was restored, but the poor little back was shockingly mangled, and vomiting continued at intervals through the night..."*

In Boston in 1645, *"the Governor's assistant was fined five pounds for whipping a young culprit unlawfully, no other assistant being present".* In September of 1639, Salem shopowner Marmaduke Perry was arrested for beating a 12 year old boy to death. The boy lived as an apprentice with Perry, who was constantly whipping him, until he hit him too hard and killed him. The boy, whose name has been forgotten, did however make medical history, for his was the first recorded autopsy in America. Who was it coined the phrase, *"spare the rod and spoil the child"?* — possibly it was my fellow Salemite, Marmaduke Perry.

Even I felt the rod in Salem, by a School Master in 1947. Larry Boudreau and I, both age 13, for fighting in the schoolyard, were brought before the principal, who had us hold out our right hands. This six foot two inch monster-master, with all his strength, slapped a whip into my palm, three times. It stung terribly. Then the beast brought the whip down full force on Larry, but Larry took his hand away, the principal tripped on the rug, and Larry ran out the door and kept on running all the way home. The principal is dead now, and Larry is a police sergeant in Peabody, Massachusetts. Unfortunately Larry missed being one of the last to receive corporal punishment in the Massachusetts school system.

Diarist Samuel Breck tells us that, when he was a boy living in Boston in the early 1700s, *"a large whipping-post, painted red, was located on King Street"*, now State Street, *"where women were taken in huge cages in which they were dragged on wheels from prison and tied to the post with bare backs which thirty or forty lashes were bestowed among the screams of the culprits and the uproar of the mob,"* and all this bloody hysteria took place just outside the windows of the school house, where children could bare witness. Even as late as 1784, there is court record of *"numerous persons whipped at the Post in State Street for various offences,"* and in 1790, over 18,000 Bostonians gathered on October 14th, to see 14 people whipped at State Street.

It seems that the Puritan fathers had few scruples when it came to beating or whipping children, or women. The English laws that they brought here with them, they often accepted or rejected at will. One English law that they first accepted and then partially rejected was: *"the infliction of chastisement on a wife by a husband with a reasonable instrument."* In other words, a man could beat his wife if he wanted to, as long as the stick wasn't too big. After a fury of wife-beatings, Governor Winthrop passed a Massachusetts Bay amendment to the law, which read in part: *"Every married women shall be free from bodily correction or stripes by her husband, unless it be in his own defence upon her assault. If there be any just cause of correction, complaint shall be made to authority assembled in some court, from which only she shall receive it . . ."* The Puritan magistrates had complaints from many battered wives. Judge Buller, having to set a precedent concerning the law, made a determination that, *"not knowing exactly what a reasonably sized instrument might be that a husband may use to strike his wife, I hold that a stick no bigger than my thumb, comes clearly within the description of a reasonable instrument."* Later that day, Judge Buller was visited by a group of Charlestown women who requested that they might take a look at his thumb.

Overtalkative, brash, or scolding women were often publicly whipped, or made to sit in the stocks or stand in the pillory for a few hours. In 1640, a Mrs. Gregory of Springfield, Massachusetts, argued with her neighbor and ended the argument by threatening to *"break her head open."* she was forced to sit in the stocks until she apologized to her neighbor. Also, at Springfield, in 1651, a Mrs. Hunter was gagged with a *"gossip's bridle"* for speaking ill of her neighbors. five years later a women of Taunton *"was whipt on market day, and have a 'B' for blasphemy cut out of red cloth and sewed to her garment on her right arm, to be worn forever, and to be fined."* At Boston in 1652, Ann Boulder was ordered *"to stand in irons half an hour with a paper on her breast marked 'PUBLICK-DESTROYER OF PEACE'."* Sometimes, if a husband wasn't able to shut up a scolding wife, he too was penalized by the magistrates: *"Margaret Henderson of Boston, on this day of 1639, is censured to stand in the market place with a paper on her ill behavior, and her husband is fined five pounds for her evil behavior and is to bring her to the market place for her to stand there."*

John Dunton, an Englishman visiting New England in 1686, wrote home to his family about the mistreatment of women in America. *"For the crime of cursing and swearing,"* he wrote, *"they bore through the tongue with a hot iron. For scolding others, they gag and set them at their own doors for certain hours, for all comers and goers to gaze at. If this were the law in England, it would in a little time prove an effectual remedy to cure the noise that is in many women's heads . . ."*

Some New England towns used a *"brank"* or *"gossip's bridle"* to close the mouths of scolding or over-talkative women. Henry Heginbotham, an English historian, describes the brank as an *"iron gag."* A cage-like device that fit over the head, *"with a tongue-plate about two-inches long, having at the end, a ball into which is inserted a number of sharp iron pins, three on the upper surface, three on the lower, and two pointing backwards. These could not fail to pin the tongue and effectually silence the noisiest female brawler."* In the larger towns like Springfield and Boston, it was used, if sparingly, into the mid 19th century.

In 1672, a new instrument for punishing women was introduced. The Massachusetts law read: *"Whereas there is no express punishment by any law hitherto established affixed to the evil practice of sundry persons of exorbitancy of the tongue in rayling and scolding, it is therefore ordered that all such persons convicted before any Court or Magistrate that hath proper cognizance of the cause for rayling or scolding, shall be gagged or set in a ducking stool and dipt over head and ears three times in some convenient place of fresh or salt water, as the Court or Magistrate shall judge."*

Every village and town, by law, was required to have on hand a ducking stool, and some communities, like Kittery and York, Maine, were fined for not constructing one. A visiting French-Canadian described a ducking-stool in Maine as, *"an arm chair fastened to the end of two beams, some fifteen feet long parallel to each other, embracing the chair which hangs between them. It is set upon the bank of a pond with the chair hanging over the water, and they plunge the woman in the chair into the water, as often as the sentence directs, to cool her heat."* The ducking stool was used more extensively in Scotland and England than it was in New England, and British historian J. Peter Briscoe relates that at Nottingham, England in 1731, *"Mayor Trigge caused a female to be placed in the stool for immorality, and he left her to the mercy of the mob, which ducked her so severly that she drowned."*

Salem, Massachusetts was one of the first towns in New England to construct a ducking stool, and although there is no record of a ducking in my home town, a replica of the stool can be seen today at Duck Pond, Pioneer Village, Forest River Park in Salem. The last recorded ducking in America was not in New England, but at Jersey City, New Jersey, in 1889 - *"Mary Brady to be dipt thrice in the stool for being a common scold."*

Besides the constant threat of falling victim of the cruel instruments of Pilgrim and Puritan justice, the first citizens of New England were burdened with a multitude of silly laws and ridiculous ordinances that were strictly enforced by the combined force of church and state. One could not wear fancy or colorful clothing without being subject to a fine or a few hours in the pillory. The Pilgrims were less strict than the Puritans on the subject of proper dress, and required that black only be worn on Sundays. The Puritans, however, demanded that their followers wear only black and dull colors all the time, *"without frills such as ribbons, bows, silks or laces."* In just one month, November 1652, no less than 15 cases came before the Salem court concerning *"the wearing of excess clothing."* Strangely enough, eight of them were charges brought against men for *"dressing too colorfully."* One of those dapper young Puritans, brought to trial by his neighbors, was Henry Bullocke. He wore *"boots, ribbons, lace, gold and silver."* For his *"fanciness,"* he was found guilty and fined twenty pounds, a heavy price to pay in those days, but apparently Henry could afford it. At Haverhill, Massachusetts, the two daughters of Nathaniel Bosworth, in 1675, were fined ten shillings apiece, *"for wearing silk."* Elizabeth Eddy of Boston, was fined only ten shillings for her clothes, but not for wearing them.. She was brought to court and found guilty of *"hanging her wet clothes outside to dry."* Only a month later, Elizabeth's mother was brought to trial and found guilty of *"fishing for and catching eels."* She was fined five shillings.

It was as early as 1628 when Cape Anne fishermen and Naumkeage Puritans argued for a day over the growing of tobacco in New England. At the end of the meeting, the Puritans had won the argument, and because they had come to a peaceful resolution, they decided to call the place of their meeting *"Salem"*, the Hebrew word for *"peace"*. Two years later at Salem, the Puritans had a new law on the books: *"No person shall take tobacco publicly, and if so, shall be fined five pounds."* Although the fine was heavy, the law was fairly lenient, considering that at the same time in Russia the law read that, *"snuffers and smokers shall be whipped, and if caught snuffing a second time, shall have their noses sliced off, and if smoking, be executed."* The Indians of New England loved tobacco, and one of their greatest enjoyments was smoking the peace-pipe at their pow-wows. The Indians believed that smoking cured many ills, and they were more than willing to pass the peace-pipe to their Puritan and Pilgrim neighbors. One of the earliest laws however, in Plymouth and Boston was that *"no one be allowed to attend an Indian Pow-Wow."* Violators were fined and made to sit in the stocks.

An ordinance passed in 1649 at Portsmouth, New Hampshire read: *"Foreasmuch as the wearing of long hair, after the manner of ruffians and barbarous Indians, has begun to invade New England, contary to the rule of God's word, which says it is a shame for men to wear long hair — We the Magistrates do declare and manifest our dislike and detestation against the wearing of such long hair."* The year before at Salem, Massachusetts, an item in the court record reads: *"John Gatshell is fyened ten shillings, and shall cutt off his long hair of his head, and in the meantime, he shall have abated five shillings his fine, to be paid into Town meeting within two months from this time, and have leave to go in his building in the meantime."*

Any Indian, servant, slave, or stranger, found walking the streets of any New England village or town after dark could be arrested on the spot by the Constable or the night-watchman. Even a person known to the Contstable or watchman of the town, who was on the street after ten o'clock at night, could be stopped, questioned and ordered to return to his home. Another law of the land was, *"anyone who fires a piece* (musket) *after sunset, shall be fined forty shillings or be whipped.* " The probable reason for this law was to avoid startling the night watchmen, the military-like night guards, who might conclude Indians were invading if they heard a shot in the night. Most communities had towers built for the watchmen to overlook the town center, and they made regular rounds about the streets, getting people off the streets and to bed. They usually shouted as they walked, *"All's Well!"*, and this nightly function carried on into the 19th century. Salem's famous diarist Doctor Bentley, once logically commented, *"wouldn't it be better for the watchman to cry out when all is not well, and let well enough alone?"*

Even Town Fathers, members of the court, and watchmen, sometimes found themselves victims of Puritan laws. Watchman William Almy of Salem, in 1641, was fined five shillings *"for taking away Mrs. Glover's canoe without leave,"* and Sir Richard Saltonstall, Town Father of Salem, was *"fined four baskets of wheat for his absence in Court."* Thomas Withers, an aspiring politician of York, Maine in 1671, wanted desperately to be a Town Father. The election was held, and Withers ended up pinned for days to the pillory. His crime, *"for putting in several votes for himself as an officer at Town Meeting."* Another criminal, although more successful than Withers, was William Veasey of Braintree, Massachusetts. He won a seat in the Great and General Court in 1697, but he couldn't take his seat on the day the legislature opened, for he was standing in the pillory at Braintree. He had been found guilty of *"plowing his field on Thanksgiving."*

Thanksgiving, Easter and Christmas were days of prayer, and no Puritan was allowed to work or play on those days. One of the first laws on the books at Salem in 1628, was the banning of Christmas. If anyone attempted to celebrate it in any way, he would be sent to the stocks, have his ears chopped off, and possibly be banished from the community. The Governor actually sent out spies on Christmas to sniff out Puritan homes for any Christmas smells. The Pilgrims were less strict about what we consider today as holidays, and of course, Thanksgiving, a day not only of prayer but of feasting, originated with them. The Pilgrims, however, were often criticized more than the Puritans by visitors to New England, who thought them cruel, harsh and inhospitable. In fact, only a few years after they settled at Plymouth, the Plantation backers in England sent Governor Bradford a letter, which in part read: *"You condemn all other churches and persons but yourselves and those in your way, and you are contentious, cruel, and hard-hearted among your neighbors . . ."* Imagine saying that about our Pilgrim Fathers? Apparently these Englishmen hadn't met *"the neighbors,"* those sweet humanitarians of Salem and Boston, who called themselves, *Puritans.*

II
NEVER ON SUNDAY

Today in New England, they are called *"The Blue Laws,"* state laws that determine what a person may or may not do on a Sunday, the Christian Sabbath Day. The Jewish Sabbath Day is Saturday, which sometimes confuses the issue in obeying God's Commandment, *"Thou shall keep holy the Sabbath."* Within the last few years the Blue Laws were, for the most part, repealed, allowing stores to open for business on Sunday. Although there are some who follow strict rules and regulations concerning the Sabbath, and many who attend church on Sunday, or Synagogue on Saturday, most New Englanders consider the Sabbath as a day of rest, relaxation and recreation. Not so for our Pilgrim and Puritan forefathers, who first planted the seeds that resulted in the Blue Laws — they lived under strict Sabbath Day discipline. In those days, the church dictated what you could or could not do from sunset on Saturday night until Monday morning, and the punishments were harsh for those who disobeyed Sabbath laws.

There was Captain Kimbal of Salem, who *"publicly and lewdly kissed his wife on the Lord's Day at noon,"* and was made to sit in the stocks for the remainder of the day. Kimbal had just arrived in port after a six month voyage to the West Indies, when his wife met him at the wharf and he kissed her — what a homecoming! Not only couldn't a man kiss his own wife on Sunday, but the wife wasn't allowed to cook, clean, or make the beds on Sunday. All this work had to be done before sundown on Saturday. Pilgrims and Puritans were not allowed to work, play, travel, write letters, or argue on a Sunday. From the Salem court records of December 4, 1638, we find, *"two Salem men sit in the stocks for travelling on the Sabbath."* At about the same time in Salem, it's interesting to note, that even non-Puritans were under the same restrictions: *"Two Indians, fined for carrying wood on the Sabbath,"* and the Indians weren't allowed to go hunting or fishing on Sunday either, without suffering punishment from the Puritans. In places like Andover and Haverhill, Massachusetts, settlers and Indians alike, were put into cages outside the meetinghouse, and were heavily fined as well, for *"breaking the Sabbath."* The Indians usually paid their fines with baskets of corn. In Portsmouth, New Hampshire, May, 1662, the Selectmen passed an ordinance that, *"a cage or some other similar device be invented in which to place those who break the Sabbath, or for those people who sleep or take tobacco on Sunday."*

Sunday services lasted almost all day, with the minister preaching to everyone in the village or town for hours on end, and God help anyone who would doze-off during those long religious lectures. Roger Scott of Salem, apparently just couldn't keep his eyes open during the Sunday sessions, for in 1643, he was caught, *"for repeated sleeping in meeting on the Lord's Day, and for striking the person who walked with him"* — he slapped the man who squealed to the minister that he was sleeping. *"Scott was sentenced to be severly whipped."* In New Haven, Connecticut, a Mister Fitch was *"fined four shillings and be whipped, for he did not hear the word of God preached by Reverend Fitch."* Apparently the two men, minister and victim, were related, which obviously resulted in family friction.

In Plymouth, the law of the Pilgrim Church was quite explicit: *"All persons who stand out of the meeting-house during time of service, shall be set in the stocks for two hours . . ."* and anyone *"demeaning themselves by sleeping or jesting, if they shall persist in such practices, shall be set in the stocks."*

A *"Tithing Man,"* or church policeman was appointed in every Pilgrim and Puritan church to: *"quiet the restlessness of youth and to disturb the slumbers of age"* during long hours of Sunday sermons. He usually carried a *"tithing-stick,"* a long tapering pole, sometimes with a fox-tail attached to the end of it to, *"brush ye faces of them that will have naps."* The crueler tithing man would attach a pin or thorn to the end of his pole, to prick the restless children, or those who slept too soundly. Obadiah Turner of Lynn, Massachusetts, wrote of an incident in his 1646 diary, concerning his friend, tithing man, Allen Bridges: *"June 3rd- Allen, as he strutted about ye meetinghouse on ye last Lord's day, did spy Mr. Tomlins sleeping with much comfort, his head kept steady by being in ye corner, and his hand grasping ye rail. And so spying, Allen did quickly thrust his staff behind Dame Ballard and gave him a grevious prick upon ye hand. Where upon Mr. Tomlins did spring up, much above ye floor, and with terrible force, strike his hand against ye wall; and also to great wonder of all prophanly exclaimed in a loud voice, 'curse ye woodchuck,' he dreaming, so it seemed, that a woodchuck had seized and bit his hand. But on coming to know where he was, and the great scandal he had committed, he seemed much abashed, but did not speak. And I think he will not soon again go to sleep in meeting."*

A boy beating on a drum early Sunday morning, summoned the citizens to worship, except in Haverhill, where in 1651, Abraham Tyler was hired for a peck of corn from each family, *"to blow his horn in the most convenient place every Lord's day, for about half an hour before meeting begins."* Once inside the meeting-house, the wealthier folks, or *"freemen,"* who paid higher taxes to the church, sat up front, usually in pews, while the poorer folks sat on benches, and the children and servants were seperated to sit in their own special place in back, under the eye of the tithing man. Negroes and *"praying Indians,"* who had adopted Christianity, either were given standing room at the back of the meeting-house, or were allowed to look in through the windows. Some meeting-houses had balconies for them. Women were often separated from the men, and either made to sit in back, or in the balcony. The Pilgrim minister in 1668, John Cotton, Jr., didn't like the idea of women sitting in his church at all. He considered females to be *"the source of all sin"*. He often criticized the women of Plymouth during his Sunday sermons for *"not teaching your children properly"*. During "The Great Indian War" of 1676, he gave a Sunday sermon, blaming the Indian uprising *"on God's displeasure at New England's women and their offspring"*. Judge Sewall of Boston, in his diary of 1697, writes that Reverend John Cotton, Jr. *"was directed to make an orderly secession from the Church by a Council at Plymouth, for his notorious breaches of the Seventh Commandment"* — the Pilgrim minister was caught playing around with little girls. He admitted his fault, and sailed off from Plymouth to North Carolina, where he died two years later. If one of his parishoners had been caught in the same horrid sin, I'm sure that Reverend Cotton would have had him flogged, or possibly hanged.

Anyone who spoke out against the Puritan church, or its ministers, was severely punished and often banished from the community, forced to either take the next ship back to England, or wander in the New England wilderness. Such was the fate of Philip Ratcliff in June of 1631. He was whipped, had his ears cut off, paid a fine of 40 pounds, and was banished from all settlements of Massachusetts Bay, *"for uttering malicious and scandalous speeches against Salem Church and the Government"*. Hugh Bewett was also banished from Boston and other Puritan settlements, because he said that he was *"free from original sin"*. From 1631 through 1636, Dorothy Talby of Salem was continuously ridiculing the Puritan ministers, and she also came before the Essex County magistrate many times for beating her husband. She told the magistrate and the minister that *"God has commanded me to do these things"*. She was often shackled to the whipping-post outside the meeting-house, and on Sundays after meetings, was publicly whipped. She had a child from her battered husband in December of 1636, a little girl, whom she appropriately named *"Difficulty"*. That same year, the Puritan ministers expelled her from the church, and hearing this, she murdered her child. *"Because,"* she told the magistrates, *"God told me to do it"*. Dorothy Talby was hanged by the neck in Boston, as Reverend Hugh Peters preached to the crowd a sermon he titled, *"Beware of False Revelations from the Devil"*.

Probably the most outspoken and rebellious minister, who ever set foot on New England soil back in the 1600s, was Welchman Roger Williams. He ministered to both the Pilgrims at Plymouth and the Puritans at Salem, but the Boston Puritan magistrates and ministers thought him to be a dangerous non-conformist. He preached the separation of church and state, and that no white man could own land in America unless he bought it from the Indians. The Boston magistrates decided to export him back to England, and they sent a ship to Salem for that purpose, but Williams, in the winter of 1635, left Salem and wandered into the wilderness to live with the Indians, thus escaping the wrath of the Puritan magistrates. He settled in Providence, founded Rhode Island, and became America's first Baptist preacher. He welcomed all dissenters from the ranks of the Pilgrims and Puritans, and allowed those of any religious conviction to settle in his little colony.

In 1650, Oliver Holmes was whipped through the town of Boston *"for being a Baptist,"* and he, with many others, went to live with Williams, as did the Quakers who were severely persecuted by the Puritans and Pilgrims a few years later. The Puritans called these seperatists, *"notorious heretiques"* and the Pilgrim governor called them *"pests"*. Not only did they reject all formal ritual, but their worse sin seemed to be that *"women could speak at their meetings"*. Massachusetts Governor Endicott wrote to Roger Williams, recommending violoence against Quakers, and suggesting to Williams that he shouldn't take them into his settlement, but Williams, true to form, welcomed the Quakers with open arms.

It is truely ironic that Pilgrims and Puritans, who themselves were seperatists from the Church of England, had come to New England to have the freedom to practice their own religions, would then, some twenty to thirty years later, scorn, torture, and even execute others, such as Baptists and Quakers, who wanted no more than they did— freedom to worship as they pleased.

Another minister, Reverend Ezekiel Rogers, 25 years a staunch Church of England preacher at the University of Cambridge, became a dissenter, and joined the Puritans. He did so, he relates in a letter, *"because I refused to read that accursed book that allowed sports on God's holy Sabbath, and I was suspended. By it and other sad signs, I was driven with many of my hearers into New England"*. He, with his followers, arrived in 1638, and settled in an area north of Salem and south of New Hampshire, which he called *"Rowley"*, the name of his parish in Yorkshire. For years, there has been an active boy's camp at Rowley, where baseball and swimming are a Sunday afternoon ritual — *"sports on the Sabbath"*, poor Ezekiel must be turning over in his grave. An orphan boy named Leonard Harriman came with Rogers to settle Rowley, and one of his descendants became the famous General Walter Harriman, who later was the Governor of New Hampshire.

Other ministers, some good and some bad, came to serve in the Pilgrim and Puritan communities. Plymouth especially seemed to have a difficult time finding a preacher that suited their purposes, and the minister, it seems, often had a hard time collecting the church taxes that, in part, paid his salary. Doctor Matthew Fuller of Duxbury, who had to pay his tax to the Plymouth church, said of it, *"The Devil sat in the stern of the vessel when that wicked law was passed"*. The minister told the governor what he said, and in addition to paying his church tax, Doctor Fuller was fined 50 shillings for making the statement. At Salem, wealthy merchant Philip English, who was accused of witchcraft in 1692, and managed to escape the witch dungeon and flee to New York, returned to Salem in 1693, but was later thrown in jail again for refusing to pay his church tax. He was an Episcopalian, he explained to the magistrates, and shouldn't have to pay taxes to support the Puritan church. *"Either pay the tax or remain in the Salem Gaol"*, the magistrates told him, so Philip English had to support the Puritan ministers as well as his own.

"Boston has four churches," wrote Londoner John Ward during a visit to New England in 1698. *"They are built of clapboards and shingles, and are supplied with four ministers — one a scholar, one a gentleman, one a dunce and one a clown.. You are fined ten shillings for kissing your wife on a Sunday here. What a happiness, thought I, do we enjoy in old England, where we can not only kiss our own wives, but other men's, without the danger of penalty"*.

Not only Sundays, but Thursdays became a holy day of obligation for the Puritans. It was called *"Lecture Day"* and was observed by all Puritans every week, beginning at 11 A.M. with a lecture from the local minister, which usually lasted through most of the day. In 1753, *"Lecture Day"* became a monthly rather than a weekly affair. Although non-conformists and those who broke the Sabbath in some way, were often tried and punished after service on Sunday, Lecture Day soon became the favorite time for most ministers to inflict punishment on those who disobeyed Puritan laws. At Hartford, Connecticut in 1650, a man named Smith had to *"stand for two hours openly upon a stool four-feet high on Lecture Day, with a paper fixed on his breast, written in Capital letters, 'AN OPEN AND OBSTINATE CONTEMNER OF GOD'S HOLY ORDINANCES', that others may fear and be ashamed of breaking out in like wickedness"*. Church records of every Puritan community are filled with examples of various humiliations and punishments experienced by church members on the Sabbath and on Lecture Day: Ellinor Bonythorne of York, Maine, 1667, *"to stand for three Sabbath days in a white sheet in the meeting house"*. June, 1659, William Trotter of Newbury, *"for his slanderous speeches was enjoyed to make public acknowledgement in church on Lecture Day"*. Although Ruth Gouch of Maine was found *"guilty of a hateful crime"*, the records didn't reveal what that crime was, but she was ordered *"to stand in a white sheet publickly in the Congregation for several Lecture Days, and likewise, one day in the General Court at Boston"*.

The creed of the Puritans was *"the depravity of man"*, and for the sinner who refused to repent; punishment by the Puritans themselves, and eternal damnation by God. It was this creed, in 1692 at Salem, that allowed those who confessed to being witches to go free, and those who refused to admit witchcraft and repent, to be hanged at Gallows-Hill. The public confession of sin, on the Sabbath and Lecture Day, before the minister and the entire congregation, began at Salem in 1630, spread throughout the Colonies, and lasted as a church ritual for almost two centuries. In 1681 Salem, we find two women, *"wrapped in white, set on stools in the middle alley of the meeting house"*, listening to a long Sabbath lecture, *"having on their heads a paper bearing the name of their sin"*. After the sermon by the minister on the evils of their sin, they then loudly admitted their sin and publicly repented.

Governor John Winthrop in his Journal gives us a good example of a poor repentant soul coming before the Puritan congregation in Boston: *"Captain John Underhill, a brave soldier, being brought by the blessing of God in his church's censure of excommunication, to remorse for his foul sins... And, indeed it was a spectacle which caused many weeping eyes... He came in his worse clothes, in a foul linen cap pulled close to his eyes, and with many deep sighs and abundance of tears, lay open his wicked course, his adultry, his hypocrisy, and especially his pride, as the root of all which caused God to give him over to his sinfull courses, and contempt of magistrates . . ."* A sad, humiliating and blessed spectacle, except for the fact that it wasn't the first time Captain Underhill had come before his fellow Puritans to confess his sins and ask forgiveness, nor was it his last. After his stirring and emotional plea to

God and man at the meeting house, he went out and committed the same sins, and returned a few months later to put on the same show.

Probably the most dramatic Sabbath confession in Puritan history, was that of Judge Samuel Sewall at the South Church in Boston, five years after he had been instrumental in sending 19 innocent people to the gallows during the 1692 witch hysteria. He handed his letter of guilt and repentance to the minister to read before the congregation, as he stood, head bowed before them. In part it read: *"I Samuel Sewall... desire to take the blame and shame of it, asking pardon of men, and especially desiring prayers that God would pardon that sin"*. Two of the other notorious "witch-hanging" judges, Hathorne and Stoughton, did not make public Sabbath confessions, and Judge Stoughton, who became acting Governor of Massachusetts from 1694 to 1698, told Sewall that he opposed his confessing.

It was twelve year old Ann Putnam Jr., who through the prompting of her mother Ann Putnam Sr., sent hundreds of people to Salem's Witch-Dungeon, falsely accused the 19 who were hanged for witchcraft, and by telling lies to the judges, caused Giles Corey to be cruelly crushed to death by the Sheriff. She was truly the leader of the young girls who caused all the death and suffering at Salem in 1692. Although there is no record of the other girls admitting guilt, Ann Putnam Jr., fourteen years later, came before the Puritan congregation after a Sunday sermon at Salem, and confessed: *"It was a great delusion of Satan that deceived me in that sad time"*, she told them all, *"whereby I justly fear I have been instrumental to bring upon myself and this land the guilt of innocent blood"*. She was also instumental in bringing about the decline of strict Puritanism in New England. Yet, even though the Salem Witch Hysteria diminished some of the powers of the Puritan ministers, strict Sabbath Day regulations, as part of the law of the land, remained in effect for hundreds of years.

Eight years after the witch delusion, Job Tyler of Andover, Massachusetts, where most of those accused of witchcraft in 1692 had come from, was found guilty and fined by the grand jury of *"travelling on the Sabbath from his home to Woburn"*. Also, in the year 1700, John Holland was fined *"for sailing out of Ipswich River on the Sabbath Day, February last"*. On November 5th, 1705, Samuel and Sarah Coleman, brother and sister, were arrested by the Constable *"for travelling on Sabbath from Topsfield to Chebacco"*. Samuel pleaded mercy for the court, stating that, *"my sister had taken ill, and having no convenient place in Topsfield to reside, and fearing she would have the distemper or a fever, I was necessitated to do so"*. The case was dismissed and Coleman didn't have to pay a fine, but he did have to pay court costs. Edward Cox of Topsfield, Massachusetts, in February, 1720, was brought to trial at Salem for not going to church on Sunday. Cox said that he was sick, and he was released, but he also had to pay the court costs. Five years later, Nicholas Cree, a seaman, was also brought to trial at Salem for missing church service on Sunday. He pleaded that, *"my clothing were lost at sea, so I couldn't go to church"*. He too, only paid the court fee of two shillings. That same year, however, John Machallum of Ipswich appeared in court for missing Sunday service, with the excuse that, *"I had no suitable clothes"*. He was fined 20 shillings, and also had to pay the court costs.

The Great and General Court of Massachusetts, in fact, intensified the Sabbath Day laws in 1727, by adding that, *"swimming and unnecessary walking on highways or in fields on Sabbath are prohibited, and violators are to be put in jail"*. The following year thay added still another restrictive clause, that *"walking on the Common"* was a violation of the Sabbath. Even into the 19th century, the General Court was passing new laws concerning the Sabbath. In 1815, the Massachusetts legislature decreed that, *"city people can not go into the country on Sundays"*. There were at this time, many Bostonians arrested for travelling into suburbia on Sabbath Days. That same year, however, the Supreme Court decided that *"neither a police officer nor a Justice can serve an arrest-warrant on the Lord's Day"*, and so, the city folks illegally visited their country cousins on Sundays, realizing that no one could legally arrest them for doing so.

The slowly changing attitudes of the people concerning church laws and the influence they have on the city, state, and federal laws, is presently an issue of debate and sometimes turmoil in America. The rebellious doctrine of *"seperation of church and state"*, exposed by Roger Williams in the 1600s, is still being argued to an even greater extent today. The clergymen of the many religious denominations prominent in America, remain influential and powerful, especially on the Sabbath, when their power comes to light. As in the days of yore, there are good clergymen and bad ones, but it seems that after the witch dilemma in Salem, when Puritan ministers literally found devils and demons at every turn of the road, and witches in every village and town, the people began to question their dictates and decisions. Sarah Emery of Newbury, Massachusetts, writing about her childhood in post-Revolutionary War days, tells about a new minister who came to town to take over the duties of the local church. She, her family, and her father especially reacted differently when the new minister laid down the law, revealing that the church still had a strong influence on their day-to-day lives. *"We had a party for the new minister,"* writes Mrs. Emery. *"The house had been thronged . . . the pantry was empty, the liquor case, ditto, and those Dogtowners had drank a gallon of new rum, and nobody knew how much cider. . . The new minister, as father and others predicted, the ordination over, a new order of things began to be initiated. During the winter it had been customary for the middle-aged and elderly people to gather at social teas, after which the hours were enlivened by a game of checkers, backgammon or cards; and the young people held evening parties where the youth and maidens tripped the light fantastic to a tune hummed by themselves, or to the notes of a fife or flute. . . The new pastor soon announced his condemnation of this innocent gaity. A series of sermons were preached which pretty effectually stopped dancing and card playing . . . Father's dissatisfaction was so great that he took a pew in the new church that had been recently built at Byfield."*

And so, with the gradual toleration of new religions in New England, if a minister became too strict in his discipline, one had the freedom to *"join the new Church at Byfield"*, where a liberal-minded minister might allow one to dance, or possibly even smoke on the Sabbath.

The three sisters of Salem; Sarah Cloyse, Mary Easty and Rebecca Nurse, (played by Vanessa Redgrave, Kim Hunter and Phyllis Thaxter in the television production "Three Sovereigns For Sarah") languish in the Witch Dungeon with four year old Dorcas Good. Photo by Mikki Ansin. The three-figured life-size statue of the sisters, by sculptor Yiannis Stefanakis, soon to be presented to Salem as a monument to all those who suffered during the witch hysteria.

III
DRUNK AND DISORDERLY

Our Puritan and Pilgrim forefathers were heavy drinkers, of that there is little doubt. Beer and wine were consumed with almost every meal, and even the children were given beer and not milk to drink. The Pilgrim Fathers, when beer, wine, or rum was available, drank every day, but usually in moderation. Like the Puritans at Boston and Salem, they did not celebrate Christmas, and considered it, as Governor Bradford tells us, *"a human invention."* Yet, at Christmas time aboard the Mayflower, only a few days after they had landed at Plymouth, the Pilgrims were invited *"to drink with Captain and Crew aboard the ship"* from a newly opened barrel of beer, in celebration of Christmas. On that day, Bradford tells us, the Pilgrims had been *"reduced at last to drink water."*

Only five years later, the Pilgrim Fathers were up-in-arms over the *"drinking and frolicking"* at the nearby trading post at Mount Wollaston, now part of Quincy and Braintree, Massachusetts. The leader of the men at the trading post, Thomas Morton, was called the *"Lord of Misrule"* by the Pilgrims. Myles Standish, who Morton called *"Captain Shrimp!,"* was sent to Morton's Merry Mount with eight armed men in 1628, to arrest the *"merry-makers"* for selling *"guns and strong drink to the Indians."* When Standish arrived at their fort, he said that Morton's men *"were too drunk to lift their muskets."* After a short scuffle, Morton was captured by Standish and shipped back to England, only to return to Plymouth a few years later and eventually settle at Watertown, where he became a man of wealth from successfully trading with the Indians. During his *"merry-making"* lifetime, Morton did get in trouble again, when he wrote a book titled: *"New English-Canaan,"* in which he made fun of the Pilgrims and Puritans. He was given a heavy fine, and spent a year in jail for writing the book, and the book was publicly burned by the Puritans.

"The multiplying of ordinaries, or places of strong drink in Plymouth, we judge to be as the digging of an open pit," said the Pilgrim minister John Cotton Jr., only some forty years after the arrival of the Mayflower. Speaking before the General Court, he argued that, *"much precious time is spent, and money lost by men going from one drinking house to another... and not only Englishmen, but Indians are greatly maintained in a way of drunkenness."* There had been an early law in Plymouth and Boston restraining the sale of *"strong drink"* to the Indians. The law was repealed by the General Court in 1656,

but the records do not reveal why. More than likely the Indians were upset at not being able to buy *"fire-water,"* and until the Great War with the Indians, twenty years later, neither Pilgrim nor Puritan wanted trouble with his red-skinned neighbor. After the Great Indian War of 1676, however, the drinking laws were strict concerning Indians. At Haverhill, Massachusetts, the law was quite explicit: *"There will be no sale of liquors to those devilish savages."* In 1683, tavern owner John Page of Haverhill was fined forty shillings *"for selling drink to Indians."* About the same time, an Indian was caught by the Constable, drinking rum in Sprague Tavern at Plymouth. The tavern keeper was fined a few shillings, but the Indian had to work for two weeks, cutting and hauling wood for the very man who sold him the liquor. This didn't make sense to the Indian and he complained to the Pilgrim Fathers, who, in their wisdom extended the time that the Indian was compelled to cut and haul wood.

Although beer and ale were brewed in the homes of Pilgrims and Puritans, usually every week, and cider and wine were inexpensive to procure, rum was the favorite drink of the Pilgrims, Puritans and Indians. From the sugar-cane of the West Indies, imported in great quantities by America's first merchant-mariners, rum became the main ingredient for such drinks as *grog, toddy, flip,* and that wonderful intoxicant of rum and beer mix, brought to life by a hot poker, called by our stuffy-conservative forefathers, *"Kill Devil Flip."* The thick, dark molasses rum drinks were favorites in the West Indies, especially desired by sailors and pirates, but the sweet, smooth, amber rum drinks, were invented right here in New England, from the cold water springs of Boston, Medford, Salem, and Newport.

When Governor Winthrop arrived at Salem and moved on to establish Charlestown, in July of 1630, to begin a new Puritan settlement, he soon realized that, *"for the lack of pure water, the graves on the hillside grow faster than the dwellings."* An Indian came to him one day from across the Charles River, with a note from a white hermit named Blackstone, who lived across the river. *"Worthy Mr. Winthrop, it grieves me to know that there has been so much sickness in your company,"* the note read, *"and that there is dearth of good water. It is not so here, but there are good springs. If you will come hither with the Indian, I will show you the land."* In September, Winthrop and his company moved across the river. With him was Thomas Dudley, who would later become Governor of the Bay Colony. Arriving at this new site, he wrote, *"There is good water to drink here, till wine and beer can be made,"* and so this new land, called Shawmut by the Indians, and renamed Boston by Winthrop, provided the sweet water for beer, wine, and soon rum.

Salem was well watered, with many coldsprings, and within eighty years of this first Puritan settlement in the New World, Salem boasted of 19 rum distilleries. By 1735, Andrew Hall of Boston, who scoured the countryside for sweet cold water springs, found them in Medford, erected a still, and started making *"Old Medford Rum"*. It was the smoothest, best tasting rum ever made, loved by farmers, fishermen and fools alike. To attest to its good taste and popularity, the *"Old Medford Rum"* Company didn't go out of business until 1905.

Not only were the taverns, pubs, and inns, or *"ordinaries,"* as they called them, quite plentiful in America's first villages and towns, but the General Court, in 1656, decreed that, *"all villages and towns are liable to a fine for not sustaining an ordinary."* The leading minister of the Puritan church, Cotton Mather, thought the law was ridiculous, and commented that, *"every other house in Boston is an ale house."* Yet in neighboring Cambridge, the Puritan minister, Nathaniel Sparhawk, thought the law was warranted, probably because he was also a Cambridge pub keeper. Some New England villages and towns had a difficult time fulfilling the law that demanded they have a pub. Concord, Massachusetts was twice admonished by the magistrates *"for not having a common house of entertainment,"* and the town was fined three shillings. From the village of Newbury in 1682, Hugh Marsh wrote to the members of the General Court that, *"Newbury, some ten years since, was destitute of an ordinary and could not persuade any person to keep it. For want of an ordinary, Newbury was fined by the County, and would have been a third time had I not undertaken it."* Hugh Marsh was Newbury's pub keeper for twelve years.

Although running a public house could be a profitable business, many pub-keepers, like Hugh Marsh, considered themselves public servants, and operated under strict rules, set down by the General Court, County officers, and Town Fathers. If they disobeyed any of the rules they could be fined or severely punished. The initial conditions of owning a liquor license in the 1600s, were: *"to sell drink provided ye take serious care to keep good rule and order in all selling. Unlawful games, such as carding, dice, slide-groat, shuffel-board, bowls, nine-pins, and billiards, are not permitted. Nor shall ye suffer to remain in the Public House any person not being family, on Saturday night after dark, or on the Sabbath days. Nor shall ye entertain as lodgers any strangers, men or women, above the space of forty-eight hours, but such whose names and surnames ye shall deliver to one of the Constables of the Town. Nor shall ye sell any wine to Indians or Negroes, nor suffer any children or servant, or other person to remain in the Public House, tippling or drinking after nine O'clock at night, nor willingly or knowingly harbor in ye house, barn, stable, or other-wise, any rougues, vagabonds, theives, sturdy beggers, masterless men and women, nor shall ye entertain persons of jolly conversation, or given to tippling."* Added as a post-script by the Massachusetts General Court was that, *"Inn keepers within a mile of a meeting house, shall clear their houses of all persons able to go to meeting."* If a man was found drunk in an inn, tavern, or public house, the keeper of that establishment was fined five pounds. There were many who frequented pubs who were more than willing to inform on a pub-keeper, for some-times they got as much as half the fine as a reward.

At Dorchester, in 1632, someone told the Constable that pub-keeper Allen was selling home-made booze after hours and getting people drunk. Town records reveal that, *"the remainder of Mr. Allen's strange water, being estimated about two gallons, shall be delivered into the hands of the Deacons of Dorchester for the benefit of the poor there, for his selling of it during times to such as were drunk with it, he knowing thereof."* One wonders what the poor would do with this *"strange water"*? Pub-keeper Issac Wilkins of Middleton, also had an informer on his premises, when he was, *"suffering persons to sit tippling in his Public House on the Lord's Day,"* and was severely fined, for *"keeping about his house a pack of cards and suffering persons to play at that game."* At Boston, tavern keeper Nicholas Rogers, got himself into real trouble in 1643, *"for his drunkenness, and for making others drunk with his strong waters."* He was stripped to the waist and whipped.

Six years later, the pub-keeper at Portsmouth, New Hampshire was fined six shillings, for lifting a mug to toast one of his customers who was about to embark on a treck into the New Hampshire wilderness. The reason was that the Portsmouth Town Fathers had recently passed an ordinance that read: *The drinking to one's health is prohibited by law."* About the same time, Joseph Armitage, who ran the Anchor Tavern in Lynn, Massachusetts, was banned by the General Court from serving any beer, wine, or strong drink. Although Armitage ran a highly successful operation, accomodating Sheriffs, Constables, and prisoners, on their way to and from the Boston and Salem jails, it seems that he enjoyed drinking with them all when they stopped at his tavern. He went bankrupt, but since he was so accomodating to the courts, the magistrates decided that *"Joseph is allowed to keep the ordinary, but not to draw wine."* Also in Lynn, one Mary Tonkin was caught seven times *"unlaw-fully selling liquor."* The unlicensed sale of liquor brought heavy fines and often jail sentences, for the seller avoided government tax revenues, and the magistrates didn't like that. Mary went to jail four times, but it seems that after each sentence was up, she was back on the road that ran from Salem to Boston, selling her home-made brew. It must have been very good stuff, for unlike her legal counterpart, Joe Armitage, Mary always paid her stiff fines, and never went bankrupt.

Brookfield's tavern keeper in 1674, was John Ayers, and he got in trouble for refusing to pay his liquor taxes. The local Constable threatened to arrest Ayers, but he still refused to pay his taxes. *"I furnish sacrament wines to accomodate the minister on all church occasions,"* Ayers explained to the magistrates, *"but many times I wasn't paid for it . . . I shall not further support the minister by paying this tax, until the minister pays his wine bill."* Ministers were not only the religious leaders in those days, but the political, and often legal leaders in the community. The magistrates weren't about to tell the minister at Brookfield to pay his wine bill, so threatening severe punishment to the tavern keeper, he was obliged to pay his taxes.

In Puritan Boston, with a pub conveniently located across the road from the courthouse, one might think that the pub-keeper, a constant companion of lawyers, jurors, Constables, and magistrates, would avoid having problems with the law, but Boston court records tell us that, *"keeper of the ordinary, William Reynolds, fined five pounds, for allowing a Jury to tipple . . . The Jury, after they went from the barr and before they had agreed upon their verdict, drank two bowls of strong drink called Grog, without the License of the Court."* At Providence, Rhode Island, where the escapees from Puritanism dwelled in the 1600s, the pub-keeper was not restricted by laws, nor was he vulnerable to heavy fines and strict punishments. The reason being that, in 1687, the ordinary, or tavern, was also the courthouse, and the tavern keeper was the chief magistrate, Judge Eleazor Arnold. During the many years that he held both positions, there is no record of anyone ever being drunk or disorderly in his pub, yet there are many instances of the magistrate deciding that the guilty persons *"shall be whipt for drunkenness."* It makes one wonder where all these guilty persons consumed all that liquor?

Many times, pub-keepers would petition the court to sell beer, wine and strong drink, *"over-the-counter"* for some special festive occasions, and sometimes the entire village population would ask that *"spirits"* be allowed for specific purposes. In 1668, Newbury petitioned the Salem Court that, *"Captain Paul White be licensed to sell wine out of doors by retail for the necessary relief of some sick or other indigent persons, and so the inhabitants may the more conveniently accomodate church occasions from time to time."* Although this request may have sounded perfectly legitimate to the magistrates, one wonders who the *"sick and indigent persons"* were who needed all this wine, and what church occasions necessitate the retail selling of wine? It sounds like there were parched throats in Newbury, and that the villagers were coyly requesting permission to have a party. Five years later, pub-keeper Nathaniel Ingerson asked the magistrates that he be *"allowed to sell beer and cyder by the quart for the time while farmers are a building of their meeting house at Salem."* His request was granted, which seems highly unusual, for one of those days Ingerson was allowed to sell beer and cider, was a Sunday. The magistrates and ministers of the Puritan Church probably gave the okay to sell beer and cider on Sunday, because they all intended to be there while the meeting-house was being built. The *"raising"* of a house, barn, or public building was a gala event in the seventeenth century, and inevitably stimulated the consumption of vast quantities of liquid spirits by our otherwise conservative fore-fathers. The church records of ingredients needed to *"raise"* the meeting house at Medford, Massachusetts attest to this: *"Consumed 715 meals, 465 lemons, five barrels of beer, 24 gallons of West India rum, and 30 gallons of New England rum . . .".*

"Training Day" in every New England village and town was when the men would march around the green or common with their muskets, pikes, and swords, *"training"* for the military defense of their community. It was also a day for much fun and frolic. Training day was usually a Saturday, once a month, or once every two months. After hours of drilling and the firing of muskets and cannons, the keeper of the ordinary would roll out barrels of beer and wine, for well deserved *"drinks all around."* As one observer of a training day put it, *"this was the occasion that drew a motley crowd of venders of all sorts of wares, mountebanks and lewd women; a promiscuous assemblage, bent on pleasure. Beyond the lines there was always much carousing and hilarious uproar, and many a poor fellow became somewhat unsteady before the day had advanced."*

Local ministers, realizing that these special days of military train-ing were also times for residents to let off some steam, they would usually stay away, or leave the village-green early. The town fathers, however, who usually held a position of rank in the militia, would often warn their troops of overindulgence before dismissing them. Many a militiaman faced severe punishment before a training day was over. At Guilford, Connecticut, the militia drummer boy got so intoxicated that he was threatened with thirty lashes of the whip from his superior officer, who also happened to be the Guilford Constable. Town records reveal, however, that the drummer boy escaped punishment, *"for he doth confess he hath drunk too much, considering he was empty and had eaten little, and being disabled, fell against the still."*

At a training day in Salem, Massachusetts in 1661, a drunken militiaman was made to ride *"the wooden horse"* for six hours, holding a jug of liquor in one hand and his musket in the other. Although used sparingly, the wooden horse was a punishment devise used by some New England militias. It was the replica of a horse, standing about four-feet high, with a pointed back made of wood, which the victim was forced to sit on with a fifty pound weight tied to each foot. Although the wooden horse remained stationary, sitting on it was very uncomfortable, and after many hours, quite painful.

As common as it may have been to see a militiaman a bit tipsy on training day, it was uncommon in the 1600s to see a women over-indulging in alcohol. Many ordinaries, in fact, excluded female customers. Yet, in 1648, it was Joseph Armitage's wife who took over running Lynn's Anchor Tavern after he was deemed *"incapable of pouring wine himself,"* and in 1645, widow Catherine Clark was authorized to keep a tavern in Salem, *"if she provide a fit man that is godly to manage the business."* About that same time in Boston, Anne Walker was *"cast out of the church for intemperate drinking, going from one inn to another, and for light and wanton behavior."* Anne was called before the Governor, *"was stripped naked one shoulder, and tied to the whipping post, but her punishment was respited."* Another keeper of an ordinary at Salem in the 1680s, was Bridget Bishop. It was there that she served, *"a new vile liquid called rum."* It was also at Bridget's tavern that *"sailors played an evil game called shuffelboard, often until very late at night."* In 1679, John Ingerson, brother of the pub-keeper Nathaniel Ingerson, accused Bridget Bishop of being a witch. She appeared before the magistrates, but was found not-guilty of witchcraft. Some 13 years later, Bridget Bishop was called to Nathaniel Ingersoll's Inn by the magistrates for an examination by them, for she was once again accused of witchcraft. Ingerson and Ingersoll both owned ordinaries, as did Bridget, in Salem, and obviously they were in fierce competition. Bridget was tried, found guilty, and was the first of 19 to hang at Gallows Hill in 1692, condemned as a notorious Salem Witch.

It was six year earlier, in 1686, that an English visitor to Boston and Salem, John Dunton, wrote home to tell his family that, *"for adultery, the people here are put to death, and so for witchcraft, for that, there are a great many witches in this country . . . For being drunk, they either whip, or impose a fine of five shillings, and yet, not withstanding the law, there are several of them so addicted to it, that they begin to doubt whether it be a sin or not, and seldom go to bed without muddy brains . . ."*

The Massachusetts law against anyone seen on the streets with *"muddy brains"* was passed by the General Court on June 18, 1645. It read that, *"he that offends in excessive and long drinking, shall set in the stocks for three hours, when the weather is seasonable."* For the 15 years prior to that law, Puritan communities dealt with drunkards in a variety of ways. In 1630, the year that the Puritans settled into the New World, Richard Turner of Salem was *"fined 20 shillings for being drunk."* Richard Turner's name shows up a few times in the court records of 1630, therefore being *"notoriously"* drunk, meant that he was seen *"in his cups"* many times, and the penalty of having to pay twenty shillings, was a stiff fine in those days. Robert Coles of Boston was fined ten shillings and *"enjoyned to stand with a white sheet of paper on his back,"* on September 3rd, 1633. The white paper pinned to his back, was a common punishment, for as the court record reveals, *"DRUNKARD shall be written on the paper in great letters, for abusing himself shamefully with drink."* A year later, Robert Coles is back before the magistrates for *"drunkeness by him, comitted at Rocksbury."* His penalty this time was, *"to wear about his neck and hang upon his outward garment, a 'D' made of red cloth and set upon white, to continue this for a year, and not to have it off any time he comes among company, under penalty of five pounds, and afterwards to be punished by the Court. Also he is to wear the 'D' outwards."* This last comment by the court clerk seems to infer that when Coles was first forced to wear his *"drunkard"* sign, he sometimes hid it under his shirt.

Four men came before the Salem Court in one day in 1639, charged with drunkenness and lying. They were; George Dill, John Cook, Mica Ivor, and Tom Tuck. Dill and Cook were *"fined 40 shillings apiece for their drunkeness, and to stand at the meeting-house door next Lecture-Day with a cleft stick upon their tongues and a paper upon their hats, subscribed for gross premeditated lying".* Tuck and Ivor were *"fined 40 shillings, and to stand on Lecture Day, but not with cleft sticks on their tongues, only a paper on their heads, subscribed for lying".* Apparently Tuck and Ivor were as drunk as the other two, but didn't lie as much. At about the same time, John Davis and William Bacon, both of Boston, were found guilty of being drunk, and were forced to *"wear a red 'D' on their uppermost garments, and stand an hour in the pillory".* In 1642, at Boston, *"William Willoughby, for being distempered with wine and mispending his time, is commited to prison, to work there".* John Wedgewood was placed in the stocks at Ipswich in 1639, *"for being with other men who were drunk,"* yet Wedgewood himself hadn't touched a drop.

William Andrews, in his *"Old-Time Punishments"*, writes about

Mark Tuck of Newbury, *"a man of intemperate habits,"* who was forced to sit in the pillory for four hours for drinking on Sunday. *"To the sensation and amusement of several hundreds of persons,"* writes Andrews, *"Tuck was seated upon a stool, and his legs were secured in the stocks, at a few minutes past one o'clock. As the church clock, immediately facing him, chimed each quarter, he uttered expressions of thankfulness, and seemed anything but pleased at the laughter and derision of the crowd. Four hours having passed, Tuck was released with a sigh of relief. . ."*

One would think that with all the problems and constant struggle of developing new Pilgrim and Puritan settlements in America, the Governors would have little time to contend with drunk and disorderly persons, yet both Bradford and Winthrop of Plymouth and Boston, not only involved themselves in community drinking problems and the punishments of habitual drunks, but took precious time to record these experiences in their respective Journals. Besides the problems of heavy drinking and unruly Pilgrims and Puritans, they also had to deal with the crews of the ships that brought settlers and supplies to the New World. Winthrop, it seems, was especially tolerant of visiting sailors, no matter how drunk and disorderly they got while on shore leave in Boston. In 1640, he records that, *"One Baker, master's mate of the ship, being in drink, used some reproachful words of the Queen. We were much in doubt what to do with him, but having considered that he was distempered and sorry for it, and being a stranger, and a Chief officer in the ship, we thought it not fit to inflict corporal punishment upon him, but after he had been two or three days in prison, he was set an hour at the whipping post with a paper on his head and dismissed".*

The following year, Governor Winthrop involved himself in another ticklish problem involving a tippling seaman from abroad: *"There fell out a troublesome business in Boston,"* he writes. *"An English sailor happened to be drunk and was carried to his lodgings by friends. The Constable, hearing of it, found him out, being upon his bed asleep, so awakened him, and led him to the stocks. The English sailor being in stocks, one of LaTour's French gentlemen, visitors in Boston, lifted up the stocks and let him out. The Constable, hearing of it, went to the Frenchman, and would needs, carried him to the stocks. The Frenchman offered to yield himself to go to prison, but the Constable, not understanding his language, pressed him to go to the stocks. The Frenchman resisted and drew his sword. With that, company came in and disarmed him, and carried him by force to the stocks, but soon after, the Constable took him out and carried him to prison, and presently after, took him forth again, and delivered him to LaTour. Much turmult was there about this, for many Frenchmen were in Town. All of them, French and English, were let go, and the Constable was repremanded for being overzealous"*. Winthrop, it seems, was more tolerant of intoxicated foreigners than he was of his own inbibing Puritans.

To punish their own into sobriety, the Puritans tried the stocks, whipping-post, wooden horse, jail, and various forms of public humiliation, but in 1655, a new device of Yankee ingenuity for punishing drunkards was conceived. It was called *"the drunkard's cloak"*. Ralph Gardner of Boston witnessed its use: *"I have seen men drove up and down the streets,"* he wrote in his diary, *"with a great tub or barrel opened in the sides, with a hole in one end to put through their heads, and so cover their shoulders and bodies, called the new-fashioned cloak, and so make them march to the view of all beholders: and this punishment is for drunkards"*. An English visitor to Boston further described this strange wooden cloak in a letter home: *"I was extremely amused to see a rare specimen of Yankee invention,"* he wrote, *"in the shape of an original method of punishment drill. One wretched delinquent was gratuitously framed in oak, his head being thrust through a hole cut in one end of a barrel, the other end of which had been removed; and the poor fellow loafed about in the most disconsolate manner, looking for all the world like a half-hatched chicken"*.

The *"drunkard's cloak"* was used as punishment for habitual drinkers well into the 1800s, but other forms of 17th century punishments mentioned here, continued only to about the time of the Revolutionary War. The *"wooden horse"* however, was occasionally brought out of the stables for intoxicated American Civil War soldiers to ride. In Massachusetts today, drunks are allowed to roam the streets, unmolested by law enforcers unless they become disorderly. Yet, up until a few years ago, drunks would spend a few days, weeks, even months in jail, usually in an effort by the police to dry them out, and hopefully help them to change their ways. Today, drunkards are replaced by dope users and pushers, and the intoxicated are seemingly content to give up their warm cell-bunks for park-benches.

Although I did accomodate drunkards a few times in the Salem Jail when I was County Sheriff, it was usually to give them a warm and dry place to stay during the winter months, but only when there was room at my usually crowded Salem Inn. Of all the drunk and disorderly persons I dealt with as Sheriff and Keeper of the Salem Jail, or discovered in my research for this book, the most interesting and entertaining was a man whom I never met, nor was he a Pilgrim or Puritan. His name continuously appeared in the Essex County jail and court records, and although he did spend time at the Salem Jail, it was 150 years before I was the Keeper there. His name was Donald McDonald, and he had problems with the law and with alcohol for over ninety years. I found two old newspaper articles that pretty well sum up his life:

<u>Salem Observer,</u> September 22, 1825 — *"Donald McDonald, reported to be 103 years of age, was brought before the court yesterday, charged with being a common drunkard, of which he has been convicted before. Donald stated that he had been in various battles of the Revolution, had sailed with Paul Jones, and was at the taking of Quebec. He was found guilty and sentenced to the Salem House of Corrections for three months".*

<u>Boston Patriot,</u> October 14, 1829 — *"Donald McDonald, who has numbered upwards of 110 years, was sent to the House of Industry on Saturday of last week, in a state of intoxication. Two days previous, he was seen about our streets, a drunken brawler".*

Although there seems to be a few years of discrepancy in Donald's actual age, it is obvious that he lived a long adventurous life; storming the fortress at Quebec, battling as a soldier during the Revolution, manning the cannons for John Paul Jones, and still brawling in the streets of Boston at age 110. Obviously it was the booze that stimulated Donald's fighting spirit, but one wonders if it might have been good old New England rum that gave him such vitality and longevity.

Photo courtesy Henry Theriault.

IV
QUAKERS MEETING HAS BEGUN

When I was a child growing up in Salem, there was a popular game we played— we called it *"Quakers Meeting"*. One of us was chosen *"the Puritan"* and the others lined up facing him or her. The Puritan would then chant, *"Quakers meeting has begun, no more talking, no more fun. If you show your teeth or tongue, you shall pay a forfeit"*. We, the Quakers, then had to remain serious, as the Puritan tried to make us laugh, or show our teeth or tongue. If the Puritan was able to make us giggle or show our teeth in a smile, we had to leave the game, until one serious standout remained in line, making him or her the winner, who in turn would become the Puritan. At the time, I had no idea what a Quaker was, and it wasn't until years later that I discovered what a serious game the real Quakers had played with the Puritans back in the mid-17th century, and that the first Quaker Meetings in America were held in my home town of Salem.

Within months of settling at Salem in 1635, Ann Hutchinson started what must be considered, America's First Women's Club. The "girls" met on Mondays at her home to discuss the sermon they had heard the day before at church. Reverend Wilson, the local minister, was not too pleased with the Monday night critiques of his sermons, and he began refering to Ann Hutchinson as a *"Jezabel"*. Ann, with Mary Dyer began their "soft-sell" of Quakerism at these meetings, and soon men were invited to the meetings. In retrospect, one wonders how Ann had the time, or the room in her home to have these meetings, for she had 15 children, and in 1637, at age 46, she had another on the way. In November of that year, at the insistance of Reverend Wilson, Ann was brought before the Governor and the General Court, for *"reviling the ministers"*. Leading the forty member court was her accuser Reverend Wilson. He had even tried to persuade court member William Hutchinson to leave his wife, but William replied to Wilson, *"I am more tied to my wife than I am to my church, and I think her to be a dear saint and servant of God"*. At the conclusion of her trial, Wilson shouted at her, *"we do cast you out and deliver you up to Satan"*. She was found guilty and her penalty was banishment from all Puritan colonies, and excommunication. She was taken to a detention house in Roxbury for three months, where the people who lived there treated her cruelly. Then her husband was allowed to take her away to Rhode Island, where exile Roger Williams welcomed her. Williams allowed all Quakers to settle at Aqudneck Island, now Portsmouth and Newport, Rhode Island, which he had bought from the Indians for some *"wampum, ten hoes, and 23 English coats"*. Mary Dyer, also banished by the Boston magistrates, followed Ann with her husband to Newport. A few other Salem families, converted from Puritanism to be *"Friends"*, as the Quakers called themselves, followed Ann and Mary to settle in Rhode Island. With them went a Salem witch, an old woman named Jane Hawkins, who had been accused of witchcraft. She was to act as midwife for the delivery of Ann's child, but the child was born dead, and was buried by Goody Hawkins that night. Word that Ann Hutchinson's child was born a monster, reached Boston. Governor Winthrop wrote, *"thirty-seven monsters she bore as God's punishment"*. When Mary Dyer suffered a miscarriage, her unborn child was also called *"a monster"*.

William Hutchinson died in 1640, and Ann, with her large family eventually moved to New Netherlands, now New York, where they lived in a log cabin in the wilderness at New Rochelle. There, she and her family were attacked by Indians. Ann and all her children, but one were murdered. Her daughter Susannah was kidnapped and lived with the Indians for many months. When she was rescued in a counter-attack by the Colonists, she begged to stay with the Indians, whose company she preferred, and Susannah echoed that sentiment for the rest of her life. A gruesome sidelight to the story of Ann Hutchinson is that two Puritan ministers, Reverend Wilson and John Cotton, professed to secretly digging up the remains of Ann's last child, once she moved away, *"and shewed the monster baby with a queer flat head to above one-hundred people"*. As one person testified during the banishment trial, *"she had broken no law either of God or of man"*.

Ann's young friend Mary Dyer, did however break a law of man — the *"bloody law"*, the Puritans called it, which read: *"Death to any Quaker who should presume to return to Salem or Boston after banishment"*. Mary returned to Salem with three of her Rhode Island Friends; William Robinson, Marmaduke Stevenson, and Nicholas Davis. They returned, said Mary, *"to testify against the iniquitous laws in force there"*. They held a secret Quaker meeting in the Salem woods, were discovered, captured, and brought to Boston in chains, Salem not having an adequate jail at the time. There, they were tied to the floor in the basement of the jail. On October 27, 1659, under guard of 100 uniformed soldiers, Mary, with Robinson and Stevenson, were led from the jail to a makeshift gallows on Boston Common. Governor Endicott, who condemned them to hang, feared that there were many Quaker sympathizers in Boston who might try to help them escape the gallows. Endicott forced Mary, with a noose around her neck, to watch her two friends swing first. When they were pronounced dead, they were cut down from the tree, Robinson's skull breaking open in the fall. Their bodies were then stripped naked by the soldiers and thrown into a watery pit on the Common. A Mr. Nichols, who lived nearby, erected a fence around the pond where the bodies were thrown, to protect them from further mutilation by the many anti-Quaker Bostonians.

It was now Mary's turn, but some in the crowd chanted to the executioner not to hang her. Her son pleaded with the Governor to reprieve her, promising he would personally escort her back to Rhode Island. Endicott finally agreed — some in the crowd cheered his decision, but most were disappointed. Mary, however, with the noose still 'round her neck, refused to climb down the ladder from her perch. *"I will not come down,"* she told the Puritans, *"until you annul your wicked ways"*. The soldiers forcibly brought her down from the gallows and the Constable announced that if she ever returned to a Puritan town or village, she would surely hang.

Mary returned to Boston the following May to preach to whomever would listen. She was escorted back to the Common, where thousands gathered to witness her belated hanging. *"I will carry fire in one hand and faggots in the other,"* preached Reverend Wilson from the hanging ladder, *"to burn all the Quakers in the world."* There was no reprieve for Mary this time. That afternoon, after her hanging, a large crowd returning from Boston to Salem, began realizing that Puritan ministers and magistrates had created a courageous martyr in Mary Dyer for the cause of Quakerism. Crossing the drawbridge into town at North Street, the bridge collapsed under their weight and hundreds were severely injured — the people of Salem saw it as a warning from God, and some believed that they had possibly witnessed the execution of a saint.

Salem soon became a nest for Quakers, and many secret meetings were held in the woods and in private homes, under the upturned noses of disapproving Puritans. An elderly couple, Lawrence and Cassandra Southwick, converted from Puritanism, allowed two visiting Quakers, John Copeland and Christopher Holder to hold meetings at their home. They also invited the two Rhode Island men to a Puritan service at the Salem meetinghouse. After the service, Holder asked the minister if he might speak. He was refused, but Holder started to speak anyway. A parishioner and local commissioner, Edmund Batter, pulled Holder's hair as he spoke, and then began choking him. Another church member Samuel Shattock pulled Batter away before he strangled Holder to death. A fight ensued, and the four Quakers, with Puritan Samuel Shattock were arrested and sent to Boston Jail. Holder and Copeland were *"whipped through Boston"*, with all the strength the hangman could command. Then after being confined for nine weeks without food, Shattock was released and sent home to Salem. Holder and Copeland were escorted to the Rhode Island border, and the elderly Southwicks, in failing health, were also sent home. Edmund Batter was the hero of the day among Puritans. He was elected to a newly organized political position, with the title, *"Quaker Hunter"*, which allowed him to break into anyone's home and arrest any occupants who he thought might be holding a Quaker meeting. He proved to be a diligent and dedicated public servant.

A hunchback, Nicholas Phelps, was the first that Edmund Batter arrested for holding a Quaker meeting at his home in Salem. Then, at Ship Tavern, he arrested twenty more for doing likewise. It was easy for Batter to recognize Quaker men, for they wore their hair longer than most and they wore their hats inside buildings. They also said *"Thee"* and *"Thou"* alot. Their belief was simple — *"faith, and faith alone, is all that is needed to get to heaven"*. No rituals, no dogma, no religious rights or wrongs, no ministers were needed, and this rankled the Puritans, especially the ministers. Arrested at Ship Tavern were the elderly Southwicks, with their son Josiah, and Samuel Shattock, who had converted to Quakerism during his nine weeks in Boston Jail. One old man arrested was William Brend. He asked Edmund Batter, *"How wouldst thou know we were Quakers?"* *"You are Quakers, for you come with your hats on,"* replied Batter. *"It is a horrible thing,"* concluded Brend, *"to make cruel laws, to whip and cut off ears, and burn through the tongue, for not taking off our hats."* Brend was stripped to the waist and whipped into unconciousness. Then he was *"shackled to the Dungeon wall, neck and heels"* and scourged every day with a *"threefold corded whip"*. The whip was made of dried animal intestines, with three tight knots that *"laid his flesh bare to the bone"*. His back was sliced open, and *"his flesh was like pulp. Under his arms, tissue and blood clotted into bags"*. Some of Brend's friends, hearing of his condition, petitioned the Governor to have the jailer arrested for torturing the old man. Instead, Governor Endicott sent a doctor to the jail, who recommended that Brend be allowed time to heal.. The jailer complied, but once the wounds healed, he was whipped unmercifully again. Angry citizens protested to the Governor. *"All Quakers should be hanged,"* Endicott told them, but they convinced him to *"release all twenty imprisoned Quakers to banishment under pain of death"*. Brend was released and went to Rhode Island with most of the others that Edmund Batter had arrested.

The Southwicks were forced to abandon their Salem home, leaving two children behind. Captain John Hathorne, who gained infamy at the Salem witch trials, tried to sell the Southwick children, Daniel and Provided, as slaves to be shipped to Barbados. Edmund Batter begged local sea captains to ship the children south; but no ship master would take them. Some neighbors protested, and the young Southwicks were allowed to remain in Salem, but Provided was *"stripped to the waist and whipped thirty lashes"*. Lawrence and Cassandra Southwick with their children, fled to tiny Shelter Island, where she and the children, but for son Josiah, died from exposure and starvation. Josiah returned to the mainland, where he was imprisoned in the Boston Dungeon and later released to be whipped through the streets of ten villages and towns. He was then banished from Puritan New England and shipped off to England. In London he received more of the same punishment, whipping and imprisonment.

At New Haven, Connecticut, a Quaker named Humphrey Norton was *"fetched and stripped to the waist, and set with his back to the Magistrates, and given thirty-six cruel stripes"*, wrote Quaker George Bishop. *"His hand was made fast in the stocks where they set his body before, and burned very deep with a red-hot iron with 'H', for Heresie."* Bishop also tells us that at New Haven, a Quaker named Mary Clark, *"her tender body ye unmercifly tore with twenty stripes of a three-fold corded knotted whip; as near as the hangman could all in one place, fetching his strooks with the greatest strength and advantage."*

After his beating in Connecticut, Humphrey Norton went to Plymouth, hoping to find potential Quakers among the Pilgrims, but he was taken into custody and threatened with whipping and a fine. *"Thou art a malicious man,"* Pilgrim Governor Prence told Norton, *"and thy clamorous tongue I regard no more than the dust under my feet... All Quakers should be destroyed,"* concluded the Governor, *"both they, their wives and their children, without pity or mercy."* In his mercy, however, the Governor allowed Norton to leave Plymouth without a whipping, and without paying his fine, which Norton refused to do anyway, and return to that *"pest ridden Colony"*, called Rhode Island. Before leaving the Pilgrims, Norton got in the last word, calling the Pilgrims' beloved John Alden many unflattering names. *"Thou art like one fallen,"* Norton said to Alden as he was booted out of town. *"A tenderness once I did see in thee, but today, ye are like a self-conceited fool puffed up with pride of his heart."* The Pilgrim fathers decided in 1657, that all Quakers who entered their territories, *"shall be driven into the wilderness"*, and in 1659, they added to the law, *"Friends shall be exiled on pain of death"*.

The following year, Quaker William Ledra, one of the twenty who was arrested and jailed after capture by Edmund Batter at Salem, wandered into Plymouth. He was arrested immediately and put in jail. After a few weeks, the Governor offered to release him, if he paid a fine, but Ledra refused. The Governor then offered to ship him to England, but he refused that too. He was sentenced to death, and shipped off to Governor Endicott in Boston. Surrounded by hundreds of soldiers, he was led to the hanging tree on Boston Common. Endicott had his drummers beat the drums loudly so that Ledra's last inspiring words to the multitude that had gathered, could not be heard. Ledra joined his fellow martyrs; Robinson, Stevenson, and Mary Dyer, in the Common's watery pit, which is now believed to be Boston's Ice Pond, where skaters frolic over their graves in the winter, and children wade and swim in the summer.

The Pilgrim Fathers got word that at Sandwich, a small village that was under their jurisdiction at Cape Cod, Quakerism was festering. They sent one George Barlow, notorious Quaker Hunter, to ferret them out — he was paid a fee for each one he found. Barlow brought along his wife, and together thay captured and tortured over thirty suspected Quakers at Sandwich. The villagers, however, soon discovered that Barlow was having more than one affair with maidens who lived in the Village, threatening their arrest if they didn't cooperate with him, and his wife was selling *"strong drink"* to the local Indians. The people of Sandwich arrested Barlow and placed him in the stocks for *"immorality"*, where they allowed three of the maidens he had molested to beat his face to a pulp. His wife was also arrested and placed in the stocks. The Pilgrim Fathers were obviously upset when they heard what happened to their Quaker Hunter, and the incident prompted the people of Sandwich, from that time forward to defy the law. Sandwich became a haven and safe asylum for all wandering and mistreated Quakers. The village of Barnstable at Cape Cod, also part of Pilgrim territory, welcomed Quakers as well, after the Barlow affair. The Pilgrim Fathers sent another Quaker-hater, Issac Robinson, to Sandwich to spy on the villagers and arrest Quakers. Robinson actually attended a few of the illegal Quaker meetings at Sandwich, but he didn't arrest anyone — he, in fact, joined them, and became a Quaker himself. Fearing reprisal and possible execution from the Pilgrims of Plymouth, he moved with some of his new found Friends to a place the Indians called *"Succanesett"*. There, he built a home and opened a tavern. Today, it is where some of the finest taverns can be found, Falmouth on Cape Cod.

The Pilgrims were having problems with converts to Quakerism in a few other of their towns and villages, such as Scituate and Duxbury.

Timothy Hatherly, who had been a member of the Plymouth General Court for some twenty years, was dismissed by his collegues, because *"he opposed our Quaker and Baptists laws"*. When he returned to his home in Scituate, hat in hand, the town folks re-elected him as a Deputy to the General Court, and sent him back to Plymouth, but the Governor refused to allow him to sit with the other deputies. To add to the Governor's problems, his Assistant Governor, James Cudworth, also from Scituate, was seen actually attending a Quaker meeting in his home town. Cudworth was brought before the Governor and magistrates. *"I am no Quaker,"* Cudworth insisted, *"but I will not persecute Quakers."* He was fired as Assistant Governor. The Pilgrim spy at Scituate and Duxbury was John Cooke. Unlike Issac Robinson, he didn't convert to Quakerism, but he did finally side with them and refused to arrest any Quakers. Cooke became a Baptist, which to the Pilgrims and Puritans, was just as evil as being a Quaker. He was excommunicated from the Pilgrim church and banished from the territory. He went off to Dartmouth, as did a few other families from Scituate and Duxbury, to settle that new community.

In other parts of Massachusetts and New Hampshire, where Puritanism flourished, the persecution of Quakers was relentless. The 1656 law read: *"A Quaker, if male, for the first offense shall have one of his ears cut off. "For the second offense, he shall have his second ear cut off."* (In other words, if he comes back into Puritan territory again, after having his ear sliced off, he'll loose his other ear, unless they decide to hang him.) *"A woman shall be severely whipt; for any third offense, she shall have the tongue bored through with a hot iron."* In some towns, there was a punishment of having the right shoulder branded with an 'R' for *"ranter".*

Anyone who offered a Quaker lodging, or even a cup of water or a crust of bread, was punished and fined for doing so. There was also a rider to the anti-Quaker law of 1656 that stated that any shipmasters *"who carried Quakers into Massachusetts Bay, would be sent to jail."* In August of that year, Quakers Ann Christin and Mary Fisher arrived in Boston from the West Indies. They and the captain of the ship that brought them, spent weeks behind bars, and then were all shipped off to Barbados. On December 22, 1662, the Constables of twelve New Hampshire and Massachusetts town banded together, signing a proclamation that read: *"All are enjoined to make rougues and vagabond Quakers fast to a cart-tail and draw them through your towns, and whip them on their naked backs not exceeding ten stripes in each town, and so convey them from Constable to Constable on your Peril."*

The first victims of this unholy town and village unification were: Alice Ambrose, Alice Andrews, Anna Coleman, and Mary Tompkins. They were escorted by the Constables and whipped through Boston, Lynn, Salem, Windham, Roxbury, Dedham, Newbury, Rowley, Ipswich, Dover and Hampton, New Hampsire, and then they finally arrived at Salisbury, *"with blood streaming down their faces and naked backs."* The men of Salisbury refused to whip them further and untied them from the cart. This was called the *"Quaker Vagabond Act of 1661,"* which replaced the death penalty.

The humane, yet unlawful decision to release the Quaker women by the men of Salisbury, only justified the suspicions of the Boston magistrates and ministers, that, as Reverend Cotton Mather announced, *"the village of Salisbury is a nest of Quakers."* Only two years earlier, a Salisbury farmer, Thomas Macy, was summoned to appear before the Massachusetts General Court for violating the anti-Quaker law. Macy didn't appear at his court hearing, but sent a letter instead, stating that, *"for some weeks past I have been very ill, and am so at present. But"* Macy continues in his letter to the magistrates, *"I am willing to relate the truth of the case . . . On a rainy morning, there came to my house Edward Wharton and three men more . . . saying they were travelling eastward, and desired me to direct them in the way to Hampton . . . By their carriage I thought they might be Quakers, and I told them to pass on their way, saying to them I might possibly give offense in entertaining them. As soon as the violence of the rain ceased, for it rained very hard, they went away, and I never saw them since. The time that they were in the house was about three-quarters of an hour. They spoke not many words in that time . . . Tho. Macy."* For *"entertaining Quakers,"* Macy was fined thirty shillings and was, *"ordered to be admonished by the Governor."* Macy didn't have money to pay the fine, and in his letter, had told the magistrates that, *"I am at present destitute."* Fearing further persecution, and a probable jail sentence for not paying his fine, Macy gathered what few possessions he had, and with his wife, children, and a neighbor, Ed Starbuck, sailed from Salisbury in an open boat to Nantucket Island, where neither Puritans nor Pilgrims held jurisdiction. There, they lived with the Indians in harmony, the first white settlers of Nantucket. The Quaker problem, it seems, was the stimulus for many settlements in New England.

The year Macy settled in Nantucket, Peter Pearson, George Wilson, and Judith Brown, *"fantastic Quakers,"* were whipped through the streets of Boston, tied to a cart, *"the executioner having prepared a new cruel instrument* (a cat-and-nine-tails whip) *wherewith to tear their flesh."* The year before, Quaker Horred Gardner, *"with a new*

- 41 -

born child suckling at her bare breast," was whipped through Boston. The cruel deed over, she knelt in the street and prayed for her tormenters.

Obadiah Holmes, in July of 1651, was severely whipped through the streets of Boston, and because of his wounds, *"for some weeks no part of his body could touch the bed for the pain of it."* He, like Horred Gardner, blessed those who punished him, after the whipping. Falling to his knees he cried to heaven, *"Lord, lay not this sin to their charge."* Obadiah had committed no sin, nor had he broken any Puritan laws when he was arrested at Swamspcott. He and two others, John Clark and John Crandall, were but visiting a sick friend, William Witter, when Constables broke into the house and arrested him and the others for *"disturbing the peace."*

Besides Wilson, Mather, and Higginson, the three most outspoken Puritan ministers fighting their holy war with the Quakers, Boston's Reverend John Norton was an active advocate of torturing and executing Quakers, as he was a few years later in hanging witches. He was, in fact, hired by the Commonwealth of Massachusetts to write a pamphlet condemning the Quakers, and as payment for his propaganda, was granted 500 acres of Massachusetts land. As payment from the Quakers for his slanderous pamphlet, two female Friends caught him at a lecture at the Puritan meetinghouse at Cambridge, and broke a bottle over his head. *"The Lord shall break you into pieces,"* cried one, as Norton fell to the floor. *"It is a sign of emptyness,"* shouted the other Quaker to the congregation, *"and not of the bottle."*

Many Quaker pamphlets and books were burned by the Puritans in Boston — in great ceremony, with hundreds of onlookers. Quakers John Reeves and Ludowick Muggleton wrote a book on their religious convictions that was publicly burned at Boston Market in 1654, and in New Haven, Connecticut, as late as 1754, a book on Quakerism was publicly burned, but first, the book was whipped by the hangman, *"forty stripes"*. Thomas Maule of Salem, was ordered to be *"whipt for saying that Reverand Higginson preached lies, and that his instruction was the doctrine of the devil"*. Maule coincidently lived in what is now known as "Salem's Witch-House", where Judge John Corwin examined accused witches in 1692. After Maule's whipping in 1669, he helped build America's first Quaker Meeting House in Salem Woods, where their secret meetings were held. Unknown to Maule at the time, was that the spot he chose to build the meeting house, would soon become known as *Witch Hill*, and today as *"Gallows Hill"*, where witches were hanged in 1692. Maule also wrote a Quaker book titled, *"Truth-Set Forth And Maintained"*, which Reverend Higginson said was *"stuffed with notorious lies and scandals"*. Maule was brought to trial again, this time for writing and publishing the 260 page book. Maule testified that, *"My name in the book does not prove the same to be Thomas Maule.* Since the magistrates could not prove that Maule did write the book, even though his name was in it as the author, a jury found him not guilty. The magistrates, did however see to it that his book was publicly burned. Even the bibles that Quakers carried when they were arrested, were burned by the Puritans.

Three of the Salem Quakers, Samuel Shattuck, Nicholas Phelps, and old William Brend, after they were arrested at Ship Tavern, imprisoned, whipped, and banished, sailed to London to obtain an audience with the King of England. Old Brend died in an English prison, but Shattuck, and a Quaker named Edward Burroughs, were granted an audience with the newly restored King Charles II. *"Sire, there is a vein of innocent blood opened in Your Majesty's dominions,"* said Burroughs, *"which, if not stopped, may over-run all."* *"Then, I will stop that vein,"* replied the King. Shattuck hopped the next ship back to Boston with an order to the Massachusetts Governor from the King, commanding him to stop executing Quakers, and to release all Quakers who were in jails. Shattuck, who had been banished from Puritan New England, *"never to return upon pain of death"*, personally delivered the King's order to Governor Endicott. The Governor, of course, was not pleased, but told Shattuck that, *"I will obey his Majesty's command."* All imprisoned Quakers were released, and there was much rejoicing in Boston, with a Quaker prayer meeting held in the Boston Market on November 16, 1661, but the Quaker celebration was short-lived. There would be no more hangings, and few prison sentences, but the whippings and persecution of Quakers by the Puritans continued for many more years.

Less than two years after the Quakers' premature celebration in Boston, John Emery was in court at Salem *"for granting food and lodging to two Quaker men and two Quaker women who were traveling at Newbury"*. The local minister said that, *"it was dangerous entertaining them, for they had plague sores upon them"*, but some of the Newburyport women took the minister to task, saying that *"your words are false, wicked and malicious"*. Emery testified that one of the Quaker women, Mary Tompkins, had *"received no substanance for the space of near forty-eight hours"*, and that *"her stomach was making loud noises."* He felt obligated to give Mary and the others food. Witness Joseph Pike of Newburyport, however, testified in court that the loud noises coming from Mary's stomach were caused by *"having the devil in her"*. Emery was fined four pounds for feeding them. On the day of Emery's trial,

May 5, 1663, Lydia Wardwell of Hampton, *"a young and tender chaste woman"*, walked into the Newbury meetinghouse, *"without a stitch of clothes upon her person"*. The meetinghouse was packed with Puritans when *"she arrived naked amongst them"*, and she was *"forcibly ejected"*. She returned to her home in Hampton, but was later arrested and brought to Ipswich to be punished for *"her naked deed"*. Her punishment, the magistrates decided, was that, *"Lydia Wardwell shall be severely whipt and pay costs and fees to the Marshal of Hampton for bringing her, Costs ten shillings, fees two shillings and sixpence."* Lydia was tied to the fencepost outside the local tavern, had her blouse torn off, and naked from the waist up, *"was severely whipt thirty stripes"*.

The problem, as the Puritans saw it, was that more and more Quakers were coming into their villages and towns, *"infesting them with fanatic notions"* and obtaining many converts. Many were shipping over from England, where they were also persecuted, but most were sneaking in from *"that sewer"*, as Endicott called it, Rhode Island, which was the Quaker haven. *"Newport,"* Cotton Mather announced from the pulpit, *"is a receptacle for the convicts of Jerusalem and the outcasts of the land."* The Connecticut ministers were so upset with Quakers filtering into their communities, spreading their *"evil word"*, that they banded together and wrote a letter to the King of England, calling Rhode Island, *"a refuge of evil livers"*. In their letter, the ministers said that Rhode Island Quakers *"make Indians scorn religion by working and drinking on the Lord's Day; and on that day they made a great canoe; and called it Sunday, by the name of the day on which they made it . . ."* Neither the King nor the Parliament was about to penalize or chastise the Quakers of Rhode Island, for they made and exported to England a sweet rum, so loved by the King and the Lords of England, that it was decided to leave the poor Rhode Islanders alone.

A new wave of anti-Quakerism peaked in 1676, when the Puritans of Massachusetts ordered all town Constables to *"search out and arrest all Quakers"*. The Quakers fought back in their humble way with, what might be called today, *"the Lady Godiver syndrome"* — nude women began parading around the streets in protest to the new Puritan law. Deborah Buffam Wilson, recently married, had a dream, which she said, *"was a sign of the spiritual nakedness of the town of Salem and of the country"*, so she walked the streets of Salem naked. A great congregation followed her, many Puritans delighting in the parade, but a minister seeing her, went for the Constable and Deborah was arrested. *"I symbolize the bareness of the Puritan church"*, she told the minister who accompanied the Constable to make sure he performed his duty. Her punishment was *"to be whipt with thirty stripes on her naked back"*.

On a hot July Sunday in 1677, at the Old South Meetinghouse in Boston, the pews cramped with sweating Puritans, Judge Sewell among them — the minister, in the midst of his long sermon — when, *"of a sudden, the devil was amonst us"*. A Constable who was in the congregation called it, *"the shape of the devil"*, but Judge Sewell recognized the intruder as, *"an apparition of a woman walking slowly up the aisle between two men."* The apparition was Quaker Margaret Brewster, completely nude, her body covered from head to toe with ashes from her fireplace. Men began shouting, women screamed and fainted, children giggled or cried in terror, and the minister was speechless. *"It occassioned the greatest and most amazing uproar that I ever saw,"* said Judge Sewell. Flanking Margaret on either side were two Quaker men, and two more followed her up the broad aisle, their hats on. *"God is displeased at you,"* she shouted at the minister, and then turning to the shocked congregation she said, *"He will show his displeasure soon."* It was many minutes before some of the Puritan men pounced on her and her male Friends, and carted them off to jail.

At her trial the next day, now fully clothed and cleansed of the ashes, a calm and pretty Margaret Brewster stood before them. No one who had been at church the day before, could testify in court that it was Margaret who had caused the commotion, for as Sewall tells us, *"then she had been sprinkled with ashes, her loosened hair straggled wildly down her neck and shoulders, her face besmeared with soot."* Even the Constable who arrested her couldn't identify her *"without her black face."* It was decided however that she should be punished, and with her four male Friends, she was *"tied at the cart's tail and whipped through the streets of Boston."* There is cause to wonder about Margaret Brewster's warning that *"a calamity will come shortly, signifying God's displeasure."* For the Puritan zest for Quakers blood was waning in favor of a new scapegoat. Some 15 years later, came the reign of terror in Salem, and the *"calamity"*, that Margaret Brewster spoke of was upon the Puritans. It made them quake!

Photo by Mikki Ansin.

V
AT WAR WITH WITCHES

The fear of witches infiltrating the Puritan communities was just as real to our New England ancestors as their fear of Quakers. Witchcraft was a rival religion. Reverend Cotton Mather wrote: *"Witchcraft is a horrible plot against the country, which if not seasonably discovered, will probably blow up, and pull down all the churches in the country."* Witches, it was believed, gained their powers through the Devil, who would only work with those who signed a pact or contract with him. The Devil would allow witches to take a form of man or beast, any time they desired, except, they could not take the forms of innocent people — that was not within the Devil's power. Therefore, if a person reported that they saw the image, ghost, or *"spectre"* of a person doing something evil, that evil doer had to be a witch and could not be an innocent person — thus, *"spectral evidence"*, as our ancestors called it, was valid testimony in a court of law, where hallucinating and lying witnesses sent many an innocent person to the gallows.

Four witches were hanged in Connecticut in 1647, the first being Achsah Young. Her crime was that she used Indian herbs to cure sick neighbors. For the same crime, Margaret Jones of Charlestown, was hanged on Boston Common on June 15th of the following year. After Margaret was accused of witchcraft and arrested, the Constables stripped her naked and searched her body for *"the Devil's mark"*, usually a wart or mole provided to witches by the Devil so that a *"familiar"* — a little animal or strange beast, could suck on it to obtain bloody-milk for survival. On Margaret's body, *"in a hidden place, she was found to have a witch's mark, a teat, as fresh as if newly sucked,"* writes Governor Winthrop.

From 1648 through '52, there were seven recorded cases of witchcraft, in Hartford and New Haven, Connecticut, and in Lynn, Andover, Marblehead, and Rowley, Massachusetts. Jane Walford of Hampton, New Hampshire, was brought to trial at Portsmouth, in April of 1656, charged of witchcraft by her neighbors. She was found not guilty, and thirteen years later she sued her accusers for slander, and won the case. This was New Hampshire's only witch trial. In Rhode Island, there is no record of anyone ever being tried for witchcraft. At Boston, however, in the same year Jane Walford went to trial, Anne Hibbins, a widow, who was Governor Richard Bellingham's sister, was hanged as a witch on the Common. Anne was a quarrelsome woman, and two of her neighbors testified that *"she had approached us on the street and guessed correctly that we were talking about her. How could she know that, but she be a witch?"* Anne Cole, a middle-aged spinster, and *"a person esteemed pious"*, began having *"strange fits"* at church service in Hartford, Connecticut. In her fits, which began occuring at home as well, she heard a strange voice *"with a Dutch accent"*. Then this Dutchman started appearing to her, *"and had carnal knowledge of me, with much delight to myself."* The Dutchman, through Anne Cole, accused many others of being witches. Two who were accused and arrested, were Rebecca and Nathaniel Greensmith. Nathaniel managed to escape from jail and flee to New York, but his wife was hanged in 1663.

It was the trial, conviction and hanging of Irish washerwoman Goody Glover at Boston in 1688, that really got the witch-cauldrin bubbling. She, according to Cotton Mather, bewitched her neighbor's children, ages five through 13, often cursing them in gaelic. *"Puppets made of rags and stuffed with goat's hair,"* were found in Goody Glover's home, which prompted her to admit that she was a witch. After she swung from the gallows, Cotton Mather announced, *"I am resolved after this, never to use but just one grain of patience with any man that shall go to impose upon me a denial of Devils and witches."* That set the stage for the horror that enveloped Salem four years later.

Salem Town was separated by only three miles from Salem Village, now Danvers, and there was an animosity then between the *"high-brows"* of the Town and the *"dirt-farmers"* of the village. In the village there was also friction over land ownership and cattle grazing rights, which led to deep rooted family feuds. The Putnams, led by their vicious, high-strung matriarch Ann Putnam, detested all members of the neighboring Nurse family, who owned a 300-acre estate bordering her own meager cottage. Then there was the problem of the children - the boys worked the farms, but the girls were given menial chores, and they were bored. Much time had to be spent at the meetinghouse, learning Puritan doctrine and listening to lengthy sermons. Fun and games were not allowed. It was Ann Putnam Jr., age 12, daughter of the vindictive Ann, who ultimately provided the fun and games that the children craved.

Just up the road from the Putnams stood the meetinghouse, and the parish house of Reverend Samuel Parris, a recent arrival to Salem Village. This was his first ministerial position. He had been a merchant in the West Indies, and with him from the Indies, he brought his wife and nine-year-old daughter Elizabeth, plus two slaves, John Indian, and his wife Tituba, who was half Carib Indian and half African. Tituba was a story teller, and knowledgeable in black-magic and sorcery. Little Ann Putnam and Elizabeth Parris became fast friends and spent many hours together being spell-bound by Tituba's stories in the parish-house kitchen. The popularity of Tituba's tales and her fortune-telling, spread throughout the village, and soon there were ten village girls and maid' servants, ages nine to 19, in Tituba's kitchen, thoroughly enjoying the fun and games of her black-magic. The game went too far, however. Elizabeth Parris started going into long deep trances, and her cousin Abigail Williams, age eleven, began acting up at the dinner table. She once threw the Bible across the room, and attempted to run up the chimney. Reverend Parris called in Doctor William Griggs to determine her sickness, and the doctor concluded that, *"the evil hand is upon her."* Word spread through the village and town like wildfire. The girls blamed Tituba for their condition, and Reverend Parris gave his slave such a beating that she confessed to being the cause of the problem. Ann Putnam started naming other local women as witches, and Constables were called out to arrest them - the reign of terror at Salem had commenced.

"With heavy chains upon their arms and legs," Tituba, with beggar woman Sarah Good, and the old sickly Sarah Osborne, were brought before the magistrates John Hathorne and John Corwin for *"examination"*. The accusing girls were in court when the prisoners arrived from jail, and a loud crowd had gathered to watch the proceedings. Tituba, a heavy-set woman, was asked by Hathorne if she was a witch, and she replied, *"I am! I go to witch meetings riding upon a stick, with Sarah Good and Osborne behind me. We ride taking hold of one another."* The courtroom was hushed with awe. Here was an admitted witch standing before them, revealing all her secrets. Her confession over, Tituba was brought back to jail and shackled to the wall of the dungeon. She remained there for over a year, and never went to trial. Her reward was that she was never again harassed and beaten by jailers, ministers and Sherrif George Corwin, who was the nephew of the judge, but her confession sealed the fate of Sarah Osborne and Sarah Good.

When old Sarah Osborne entered the courtroom, Ann Putnam, with her mother's prompting, accused her of tormenting the girls. Then all the accusers began screaming that Sarah, in specter form, was pinching and biting them. They rolled on the floor, screeched, babbled and trembled, an act they would perform many times before the witch hysteria was over. There was great confusion in the courtroom, and many of the spectators loved it — some were frightened almost out of their wits. This was enough to convince Judge Hathorne that Sarah

Osborne was guilty. She was returned to the damp Witch Dungeon beneath the jail and, because of ill health and harsh treatment, ten days after her examination, she died.

The third victim, Sarah Good, swaggered into the courtroom, sticking out her belly to show the magistrates that she was pregnant. She was only in her mid-thirties, but looked seventy-years-old. She was ragged and dirty and survived with her four-year-old daughter Dorcas by begging in the streets. *"She is indeed a miserable witch,"* commented Reverend Nicholas Noyes, Puritan minister of Salem Town. She told Hathorne that, *"it is Osborne who torments the children, not me,"* but trying to pass-the-buck didn't save Sarah Good. Her husband, who left her months before, testified that, *"I may say with tears, that she is an enemy of all good."* Even little Dorcas Good, called upon to testify against her mother, said, *"my mother has three birds, and they do hurt the children."* Sarah went back to jail and was chained to the dungeon floor, but even in her suffering, continued to beg tobacco for her pipe from the jail guards. When it came time for delivery, her child was born in the dungeon — dead.

The cold, foul-smelling Witch Dungeon was where the most dangerous criminals were usually kept in chains. It was infested with disease, and being near the banks of a tidal river, it was the stomping ground for large water-rats. The little food the prisoners got, which they had to pay for themselves or starve, was often rotten, and the drinking water was putrid. John Meyforth, a scholar of the time, wrote that, *"the prisoners are fed only on salted foods, and all their drinks are mixed with herring-pickle. No drop of pure unadulterated wine, beer, or water is allowed them, but raging thirst is purposely kept up in them."* Many of the accused witches went into hysterical fits while lingering in the dungeon, and theirs were not feigned fits, like those of their accusers. The constant mistreatment and torture suffered by the prisoners from the Sheriff and his men, also took its toll. The women were periodically stripped of their one set of clothes, as jailers meticulously searched their unbathed bodies for Devil's marks. Sheriff Corwin was reminded by the magistrates that, *"the Devil's mark, being pinched, will not bleed, and be often in their secretest parts, and therefore require diligent and careful search."* The examiners carried pins with them to prick warts, moles, or pimples they found on the witches.

Various forms of torture, mental and physical, were used at Salem's Witch Dungeon, out of sight of witnesses, and mainly to gain confessions. In the Essex County court records, written beside the names of a few who confessed to being witches, was the statement by the clerk, *"the prisoner confessed without torture."* — apparently these were the exceptions. John Proctor, while awaiting execution in the dungeon, revealed that, not only were suspected witches tortured, but members of their families as well. The two young sons of accused witch Martha Carrier, Proctor said, *"would not confess anything till they tied them neck and heels and the blood was ready to come out of their noses. Tis credibly reported this was the occasion of making them confess, but they never did."* Mary Tyler of Andover said that when she was brought to Salem, *"they kept telling me that I must be a witch, since the afflicted accused me. I told them that I was no witch. I was carried to a room where my brother Bridges on one side, and Mr. Emerson on the other, told me I was a witch, and said Emerson would attempt with his hand to beat the Devil away from my eyes. They so urged me to confess that I wished myself in any dungeon rather than be so treated."* The popular torture of the time, to prove a person a witch or not, was to *"have the right thumb tied to the big toe of the left foot. Then the victim is thrown into a pond. She be innocent if she sinks and drowns, guilty if she floats."* As ridiculous as this sounds, this punishment was used to discover witches in Connecticut. It was also used in Europe, but Cotton Mather suggested it not be tried at Salem, *"for it is the invention of Catholics and Episcopalians."*

The fear of the Sheriff and his jailers was the common belief that a witch could easily escape from jail with the help of the Devil, changing shape into a small animal or strange beast that could fit through the keyhole of the jail door. A few accused witches did escape, including Salem's most prosperous merchant, Philip English and his wife Mary, John Alden, son of Plymouth's famous John Alden, Mary Bradbury of Salem, and Mrs. Cary of Charlestown. It wasn't the Devil, however, who assisted in these escapes, but family and friends of the victims. They usually paid the jailers who allowed them to flee. Most went to New York, where they were offered asylum. Captain Nathaniel Cary, husband of an accused witch, gave the jailer his life savings to free his wife. *"I was extremely troubled at the inhuman dealing of Judge Hathorne and the jailers,"* he reported years later. *"The jailer put irons on my wife's legs, and placed her in a jail room without a bed. The weight of the irons was about eight pounds. These irons and her other afflictions, soon brought her into convulsion fits, so that I thought she would die that night."* The accused witch Ann Foster did die in the dungeon, but the jailer made her son pay *"two pounds, sixteen shillings"* to him, before the son was allowed to take his mother away for a decent burial.

All prisoners at Salem's Witch Jail & Dungeon had to pay for the cuffs, chains and fetters they wore, *"seven shillings and sixpence apiece."* The Jail Keeper was also paid by each accused or by her family, *"two pounds and eight shillings."* A bit extra had to be paid for inspecting for warts and moles. Court costs were *"one pound, ten shillings apiece,"* and if executed, there was a sizable hangman's fee. The salaries and expenses of magistrates, clerks, guards, jailers, Constables and the Sheriff, were all paid for by the victim, family or friends, making witch hunting one of the most lucrative businesses of the late 17th century.

Many followed Tituba and Sarah Good to the dungeon. Joining them on April 3, 1692, was four-year-old Dorcas Good. It was 17-year-old Mercy Lewis, the Putnam's maid servant, who had accused the child of witchcraft. *"I saw the apparition of Dorcas Good, who almost choked me and she tortured me most greviosly,"* Mercy testified in court. *"She hath several times tortured me by biting and pinching."* In the dungeon, Sarah Good prompted her daughter to admit to being a witch, knowing that those who confessed were not executed, but those who insisted they were innocent, went to Gallows Hill. Dorcas remained in the dungeon for one year. *"She was a good-looking little girl,"* wrote witness Robert Calef, *"but was sent to the Dungeon, and after spending a year there, was never considered good-looking again."* Little Dorcas, after loosing her mother on July 19th when she was taken to hang with four others at Gallows Hill, went insane.

Sharing the spotlight in court with Dorcas Good, then sharing the hanging tree with her mother three months later, was 70-year-old Rebecca Nurse, hated neighbor of the Putnams. She was a saintly woman, an avid church-goer, but the girls, with their testimonies and courtroom antics, managed to get her executed. Rebecca's two younger sisters, Sarah Cloyse and Mary Easty, also when to the Witch Dungeon, accused of witchcraft by the Putnams. Sarah Cloyse, the fiestiest of the trio, stomped out of a sermon by Reverend Parris at Salem Village meetinghouse, slamming the door behind her. The afflicted girls then accused her of being *"The Devil's diciple."* At her *"examination,"* Ann Putnam and two of her girlfriends rolled on the courtroom floor, making hideous noises and shouting that they saw Sarah *"at a meeting of witches."* Even John Indian, Tituba's husband, got into the act, saying that *"Goody Cloyse choked me and brought me the Devil's book to sign."* He then went into fits, copying the girls. *"You are a grevious liar,"* shouted Sarah Cloyse, but the Indian slave and the afflicted girls sent Sarah to jail. Yet, possibly because of her fighting spirit, the magistrates never got around to executing her. Mary Easty however, the mother of seven children, was hanged at Gallows Hill on September 22, 1692, with seven other innocent neighbors.

The jails of Salem, Ipswich, and Boston were overflowing with witches when the new Royal Governor of Massachusetts, Sir William Phips arrived from England in May, 1692. He set up a new trial court of *"Oyer and Terminer,"* meaning *"hear and determine,"* then he rushed off to the Canadian border to fight the Indians. Deputy Governor William Stoughton was the new Chief Justice, with seven other new judges to assist Hathorne and Corwin. The Governor's special court met in Salem on June 2nd, to try accused witch Bridget Bishop. Like Goody Glover of Boston, *"puppets stuffed with rags and animal hair"* were found in her cellar, and she was hanged on June 10th at Gallows Hill. After her hanging, one of the newly appointed judges, Nathaniel Saltonstall, resigned, stating that, *"I am not willing to take part in further proceedings of this nature."*

Cotton Mather announced, *"An army of Devils is horribly broke in upon Salem, which is their center."* One accused witch-wizard, William Baker, announced to the court that, *"the Devil told me that near the Salem Village Meetinghouse, there are about one-hundred and five young men with knives and swords, called by Bridget Bishop and George Burroughs. Their design is to destroy the village, destroy the church of God, and set up Satan's Kingdom."* Cotton Mather responded, shouting from his pulpit, *"This means war"* - war with the witches.

Sarah Churchill, 19-year-old servant to 80-year-old George Jacobs, accused him of being a witch-wizard, after he called her, *"a witch bitch."* During his trial, he pleaded on bended knees to the magistrates that he was innocent and should not be punished, but he was found guilty and sent to the dungeon to await execution. Hearing the verdict, Sarah Churchill had a change of heart. She went to Reverend Noyes to confess that she had been lying about her employer. Noyes wasn't interested — *"Are you lying now, or were you lying then?"* he asked, then walked away from her. Sarah's nine afflicted girlfriends didn't like her attempt to spoil their fun, so they threatened her that they would next accuse her of witchcraft. Sarah changed her mind again, and old George Jacobs was hanged.

Mary Warren, age 19, another servant girl, worked for the Proctor family of Salem Farms, now Peabody, Massachusetts. Her boss John Proctor was so upset at her accusing his neighbors of witchcraft that he threatened he would *"beat the Devil out of her with a cudgel,"* and that all the girls *"should be taken to the whipping post."* Shortly thereafter, the Sheriff arrived at the Proctor farm to arrest John's wife Elizabeth for *"sundry acts of witchcraft."* John protested and tried to stop the Sheriff from taking her to jail, but he was arrested, too. The exuberance that Mary Warren must have felt after displaying an almost magical power that wisked away her hated employer was short lived. As the Proctors' maid-servant, the court placed her in charge of the five Proctor children, the youngest being only three-years-old.

The Sheriff and his deputies returned to the Proctor farm. They seized and took away all movable property, including livestock and provisions. Sheriff George Corwin *"threw the beer out of the barrel and carried away the barrel. Emptied a pot of broth and took away the pot,"* Mary Warren complained to the magistrates. *"The Sheriff left nothing for me to support the children."* Everything George Corwin collected from the homes of convicted witches he kept or sold, and in the process, he became a fairly wealthy man — these, he believed, were the spoils of war.

George Burroughs was sitting down to dinner at his home in Wells, Maine, eighty miles from Salem, when the Sheriff and his men broke in on him and placed him under arrest. He was escorted back to Salem in chains. He had been the minister at Salem Village before Samuel Parris, and his servant girl then had been Mercy Lewis. She was now 17, and had many a fantastic tale to tell about George to the magistrates. Reverend Burroughs had been married three times, and one of his wives had died while he was minister at Salem Village. Mercy charged him with murdering her. The trial of a Puritan minister and a Harvard graduate to boot, brought a standing-room only crowd to the courthouse in Salem Town. Even the renowned Cotton Mather showed up, afterwards commenting that he thought, *"it was a fair trial."* Mather, riding a white horse, was also present at Burroughs' hanging. Hands cuffed and legs chained, Burroughs was placed on the hangman's ladder beneath the hanging tree, where he recited the Lord's Prayer without fault, something a witch wasn't supposedly able to do. Some of the spectators considered it proof enough that Burroughs wasn't a witch. Cotton Mather soothed their doubts by saying, *"the Devil is most dangerous when appearing as an angel of light."* Hangman George Corwin shoved Burroughs off the ladder. Dangling with him from other branches, were John Proctor, John Willard, George Jacobs, and Martha Carrier. Cotton Mather, it seems, delighted as much in the hanging of Martha Carrier as he did in the execution of his fellow minister. *"This rampant hag,"* Mather said of Martha, *"is a person whom the confessions of the witches, and of her own children*